Hulme Generations

My great-grandfather, William Atherton, was born in 1816 somewhere in Cheshire. He and his family settled in the Hulme district of Manchester when he was a very young boy, at Ferneleys Buildings, off Chester Road and near Knott Mill. We believe that one of his parents came from well-to-do people, but why William's mother and father brought their children to live in Manchester is a mystery.

As time went by and William grew up, he met and married Miss Jane Broster. Their wedding was at the Manchester Cathedral Church on 26th September 1840 and they began their early married life in Arthur Street, Hulme. When I was a little girl, I thought people were really posh if they had been married at the Manchester Cathedral; little did I know it was then almost the only church. Apart from St George's on Chester Road, all our local churches were still to be built.

Before she married, Jane had lived at Bradshaw Court, again off Chester Road, and according to their marriage certificate William's father was employed as a mechanic and Jane's as an engineer. As their married life progressed they had several children, losing some of them whilst quite young, but one of them was to be my grandmother, and she was christened Jane Broster Atherton. (Apparently it was the done thing in those days to carry the wife's maiden name forward.)

Great-grandfather Atherton lived to a ripe old age and eventually, having outlived Great-grandmother, he rented a room in a house on Clopton Street, towards the City Road end. Many years later my mam's sister, Aunt Alice Jemima, rented the whole house.

Grandma Jane Broster, as we all called her, was the youngest of the family and had several older brothers, though we only knew of three, for as the years passed and they all grew up and married, they moved out of Hulme. Herbert, the eldest, and his wife used to run a pub on City Road, but after a short while they decided to emigrate to America and as far as we know, never returned. The next brother, Albert, had a fishing tackle shop on Ashton New Road near to Philips Park. Last but not least, there was George, Grandma Jane Broster's favourite and the only one she kept in touch with. He was an apothecary and lived over towards Moss Lane. I can still remember the bottles his pills came in; they were labelled "Atherton's Backache Pills" and there was a picture of Great Uncle George on the bottle. There would be about twenty bottles on a card, and these you would see hung up in the local grocers' shops.

On 8th June 1867, when Grandma Jane Broster was 18, she married a local lad named Thomas Jones, again at the Manchester Cathedral Church. They also started their married life in Hulme, this time in Hamilton Street, off Great Jackson Street. Thomas had been born in this street and his immediate family still lived there; no doubt this helped them to get their first home. Manchester was the heart of the cotton industry, so it is hardly surprising that Thomas worked in the warehouse. He was employed as a cordmaker, whilst Grandma Jane Broster was a braidmaker.

Grandma Jane Broster and Grandad Thomas had twelve children to their marriage and my mother, Mary, was the tenth. The first four were born in Hamilton Street, then they moved to live at No.4 Howard Street, where they had their remaining eight children. But diphtheria was rife in those days and four of the children died very young. When Ada Broster, the youngest, was born the eldest child was 23! Sadly, when Ada was only two, Grandad Thomas died quite suddenly.

Things had never been easy for Grandma Jane Broster, but with eight children to bring up alone (although a couple of the older ones still helped then) life hard. My Duke Stree Street until of twelve, start work in the mill. To make ends meet, Grandma Jane Broster had taken to "knockin' up" in and around Hulme. For a charge of 3d (about 1½p) she would be out of her house at 5.00am (or earlier for some folk), going round the streets with her long pole and rattling on the bedroom windows, wakening people for their work. This job was seven mornings a week, all the year round, in all sorts of weather.

Mam told me in later years that before 1909 there was no such thing as a pension. When people were too old to work they had to depend on their sons or daughters to help them get by, and often these were struggling to feed their own children. If things got very bad, or if people had no family, they would have to go into the Workhouse (now part of Withington Hospital). These were reputed to be very harsh and strict places, which the old folk feared. After 1909 a pension was brought in; a single person got 5s (25p) and a married couple 7s6d (37½p). This, with a little help from the family, enabled the old folk to live their lives out in peace, avoiding the Workhouse.

Some time after my mam had started work, a fair came to Hulme. Mam was coming home from the mill one evening and passed a group of people coming from the fair who had evidently had a drink or two. One of them tossed the bottle over his shoulder when he had finished and it caught Mam on

City Road in the early 1900s

the side of her head. In those days each bottle had a glass alley in the neck and they were quite heavy. As the months passed, Mam became deaf in that ear; apparently the blow had caused some damage to the inner ear and it couldn't be rectified.

Mam grew up and eventually met my father Joseph Hopkinson, who came from the Oxford Road area. His too was a large family and there were eight children in the home. According to my dad's birth certificate, he was born at Bootle. Why, we do not know; as far as we were aware, his family had always lived in Chorlton-upon-Medlock. Again, a sad story. Dad's father, Henry Hopkinson, had died while all the children were quite small and his mother, Mary Ann (nee McCabe) had a hard time of it, bringing eight of them up on her own. I remember her much later on, when all the children were grown up and married, lodging at a Mrs Thornton's off Hyde Road in Gorton.

Mary Ann's mother, my great-grandmother, owned one of those big houses which used to stand on Devonshire Street, near All Saints Park. I can recall she had a brass plate on the wall at the side of the front door, and whenever I passed the house as a child, I could not resist ringing the doorbell, only to turn and flee as if my life depended on it. Luckily for me, I was never caught by Great-grandmother McCabe!

Apparently she was quite a tiny lady, only just over four feet tall, and for some reason she had several mattresses piled one on top of the other on her bed. My dad told me that when he used to visit his grandmother at All Saints, there was a table at the side of the bed, under the lace cover of which Great-grandmother kept silver and sovereigns. Dad always tried to feel for the sovereigns when his grandmother was not looking, just out of devilment, for he was always honest. One day his grandmother caught him and slapped down hard on his knuckles. Needless to say, he never tried that again! Great-grandmother was a very strict lady and demanded respect. She was devoted to St Augustine's RC Church in Chorlton - upon - Medlock and rumour had it that when she died she left her money to the church.

Another favourite story of my dad's was to do with his "playing wag" from St Augustine's RC School. In those days the attendance officer sent to the homes of children who were absent a lot was commonly known as "the School Board". Usually somebody would spot the School Board on his way and Dad would find a hiding place. He said the best was in the drawer in the bottom of the kitchen dresser; he would climb in, get somebody to close it and escape once more. Good job he was never forgotten! We never knew if his parents found out what he was up to.

On 25th May 1907 my parents were married at St Michael's CE Church on Lavender Street, Hulme; Dad was a Roman Catholic but he married Mam in

Mary V Hopkinson

her church. Uncle John, Mam's older brother, gave her away. It was third time lucky - Mam told me in later years that the wedding had to be postponed twice owing to family illness. Their first home (I think that Dad's mother - "Ninny McCabe", as we called her - had some connection in them getting it) was a "dwelling house" on Marsland Street, Hulme, almost opposite the Macintosh, later known as Dunlop's Rubber Works, on Cambridge Street. There were four houses to each block, but they only stayed a few months because the dwellings were infested with rats and as Mam was expecting me, Grandma Jane Broster wanted her somewhere safer.

Living in Howard Street

A word to the landlord from a relative in those days used to move mountains and Grandma Jane Broster managed to get them No.12 Howard Street. I was born at this address, the eldest of their four children. In later years, as my brothers and sister were born, a neighbour used to assist at the births, but whether she was at mine I am unable to say. I was christened on Sunday, 17th May 1908, at St Michael's. Mam believed in early christenings; she used to say the baby "came on" better, and of course the mother had to be churched.

No.12 Howard Street was a simple two-up and two-down house with a lobby (some houses did not have one). Outside in the street there was a gas mantle fixed on the wall between our house and the next. When it was lit by the gas man in the evenings, it

St Michael's Church in later years

would send a rosy glow over the street. Mam always kept the house spotless, and when I think back No.12 could be classed as quite posh! In the parlour was a fireplace which had to be black-leaded and which had brass fire irons in the hearth. The furniture comprised a leather chaise longue, two easy chairs and a sideboard (they used to be called chiffoniers) which had three mirrors on top and six drawers underneath. There was also a small drop-leaf table which held the gramophone and in front of the window stood a rocking chair and a small table with a plant on it. (More about that later.) Mam had oilcloth plus a carpet and I can still see now the three sets of pictures on the wall. On the mantelpiece and sideboard were glass shades, each with a china figurine underneath.

The kitchen had cupboards fixed in the wall recesses and next to the fireplace was a large oven. Steel fire irons and a copper kettle on a stool sat in the hearth, which was surrounded by a steel fender. There was a couch similar to the one in the parlour, a kitchen table and four chairs and a dresser holding more glass shades. The floor was again covered by oilcloth and a carpet, with a small rug near the fireplace.

Off the kitchen was a tiny scullery with a sink and wringing machine, a door which led to the cellar and one which led out into the back yard where the toilet was.

The front bedroom had a dressing table with a mirror, a set of three drawers, the bed and two upright chairs. Once more, oilcloth covered the floor, as in the back bedroom, which also had a dressing table with a mirror and a set of drawers as well as the beds. Until the war Mam always had lace curtains at all the windows and each room had its own gas mantle.

They were such a friendly lot of people living in the street; I can still see them, as if it were only yesterday. On the opposite side to our house, on the corner of Howard Street and Great Jackson Street, stood the White Lion Hotel, in those days known as "Joe's Pie Shop". The first house,
No.3 was occupied by Mr and Mrs Kennerley; they had three sons and two girls.
No.5 Mrs Mooney had two sons; she lost a brother in the war.

No.7 Mr and Mrs Thompson had 3 sons and 2 daughters. One daughter, Lily, was my friend.

No.9 Mr and Mrs Makin had 4 sons and 5 daughters.

No11 Mr and Mrs Cottrell had 4 sons and 4 daughters. One daughter was born the same day as my sister Edna.

No13 Mr and Mrs Sweeney had 4 sons and 2 daughters.

No15 Mrs Carmichael had 2 sons and 1 daughter, but Mrs Carmichael's niece and her family also lived there.

No17 Mr and Mrs Moran had a son and a daughter.

No19 Mr and Mrs Carol had no children.

No21 Mrs Bowers had one son and 4 daughters.

No23 Mrs Shenton had 3 sons and 4 daughters.

(There was an entry here.)

No25 Mr and Mrs Sullivan, who had 3 sons and one daughter.

No27 Mr and Mrs Burrell had 4 sons and one daughter.

No29 Mr and Mrs Johnston had 3 sons and one daughter.

No31 Mr and Mrs Foy had 4 sons and a daughter.

No33 Mrs Stacey had 2 sons.

No35 Mr and Mrs Ward had two sons.

No37 Mrs Harford had two daughters.

There was an entry between Mrs Harford's house and the shop on the corner of Howard Street and Clopton Street, where Mr and Mrs Mallory, their son and two daughters lived. Every other house on this side of the street had a box room.

On our side, there was a shop on the corner of Howard Street and Great Jackson Street and the first house was
No.4 Grandma Jane Broster

Mary and Joseph Hopkinson with Mary and brother Joe

No.6 Mam's sister, Aunt Alice, and her family.

No.8 Miss Lizzie Bardsley, her uncle and brother.

No10 Mr and Mrs Brindley, who had one son.

No12 Our house

No14 Mr and Mrs Maguire had 3 sons and 2 daughters.

No16 Mr and Mrs Dexter had no children.

No18 Mam's brother, Uncle Ellis, and his family.

No20 Mr and Mrs Doyle had no children.

No22 Mr and Mrs Papworth (no children).

No24 Miss Andrews.

No26 Mrs Winter had 2 sons and 2 daughters. One daughter, Dolly, used to be in my class at school; she died quite young from consumption.

No28 Mr and Mrs Povah had 2 sons.

No30 Mr and Mrs Wright had four daughters.

No32 Mr and Mrs Appleton had 5 sons and 2 daughters.

No34 Mr and Mrs Ford had one daughter.

No36 Mrs McGowan had one son and 5 daughters.

The pub called the Clopton on the corner of Howard Street and Clopton Street was run by Mr and Mrs Connolly, who had one daughter and three sons. Two of their sons, the eldest and the youngest, took the priest-

The wash-house and baths on Leaf Street

hood. They were good, hard-working people who would always lend a hand should it be needed. Considering how small our houses were, it was surprising that everybody fitted in, but we all did!

I can remember being taken by my mam to City Road School (now a further education centre) to put my name down on the roll. It was only round the corner from where we lived, but we were told they were not taking any more children. So my first and only school was Duke Street Primary, the one Mam had attended herself; it too is a further education centre these days.

From the beginning I loved school and apart from illness I was never late or absent. I

Cousin Billy Jones

Cousin-in-law Maggie Jones with her son

enjoyed all my lessons and I suppose I was classed as quite bright. I won certificates for growing the best plants, and to this day I wonder how I did it, as I like neither plants nor flowers. One teacher I have never forgotten, and I don't think the other children in the class will have done either. She was called Miss Vipond and we used to live in fear of anybody upsetting her, because when she did lose her temper, anybody who did the slightest thing which displeased her would be smacked. One day Susie, one of my friends in class who lived near me, had been smacked for something trivial. Susie did no more than run home and come back with her mother! Fun and games followed. It was like watching a picture! Susie's mother, who was renowned for her temper, chased Miss Vipond round and round the classroom, until eventually Miss Vipond escaped by locking herself in the teachers' room. I dread to think what would have happened had Susie's mother caught her.

We had pencils and books; pen and ink came later. One day each week the class would be taken to Leaf Street Baths, but I never succeeded in learning to swim because of my fear of water, a fear which has never left me. Another day the class would be taken to Alexandra Park in Moss Side to play rounders. They were such happy days, even though on all our outings we had to walk everywhere. One of the songs from school which I have never forgotten was always sung on 24th May, which was Empire Day. This is how it went:

What is the meaning of Empire Day? Why do the cannons roar?
Why does the cry, "God Save the King!" echo from shore to shore?
Why does the flag of Britannia flow proudly from shore to shore?
Why does old England gladly shout on glorious Empire Day?
Where has our Empire gone?

Just after I started school I became ill and the doctor was sent for, Old Doctor Burke. In using the term "old" I am not being disrespectful; he was always known as Old Doctor Burke to distinguish him from Young Doctor Burke, his son, who worked with him in later years and eventually took over the practice. The surgery was at No.100 City Road. No appointments in those days - you just sat and waited and waited and waited. Occasionally another doctor would assist Old Doctor Burke but on the whole he worked alone. The official hours were 9.00 to 10.00am, 2.00 to 3.00pm and 6.00 to 8.00pm, but he would always be being called out, and of course he had to visit people who could not get into the surgery. Really, he never closed and he was a truly remarkable man and very respected.

The surgery itself was quite dismal, with wood-panelled walls broken only by very small windows about three-quarters of the way up. Straight backed chairs went around the room and the dispensary was at one side, with a door like the ones used in a horse's stable;

Christmas Morning, Wood Street Mission, 1913

the top half opened whilst the bottom half stayed shut. When you had seen the doctor, the prescription was made up on the premises by Miss Igo, who would open the door to take your prescription and then close it. When it was ready, she would open the door again and call your name.

Back to my story: I had caught scarlet fever and because I was so poorly, Old Doctor Burke said I must go into Monsall Hospital, which was - and still is, I believe - the hospital for any contagious diseases. I was wrapped in a huge red blanket to await the ambulance. When it arrived, pulled by two huge

horses, I was taken out to it to start my journey. The children from our street, and from many other streets we passed on the way to Monsall, ran alongside the ambulance for as far as they dared. This was the normal custom, but the noise did not do anything for the sick person inside! It was a wonder the horses never bolted, listening to all the screams and yelps from the children. Comical, though, when I think back.

That was the first of many illnesses I had. My mam used to say, "The wind has only to blow on you and down you go with something else!" The kettle was always boiling to alleviate croup, another of my ailments. Mam's remedies for our minor ills were always based on "The Oils" - that is, camphorated, olive and castor. Syrup of figs was another "bound to cure" bottle and in later years Scott's Emulsion took over. Grandma Jane Broster believed goose grease cured everything; of course, there was no National Health Service then and if you consulted the doctor, he had to be paid one way or another.

On Great Jackson Street near to City Road end there was a Police and Fire Station and another daft thing we children used to do was to follow the fire engine whenever one came out. Remember, this was before motor engines were installed; the fire engine was pulled by horses and we could just about keep up with them. It did not matter where they went, we followed, safe in the knowledge that they would return to Great Jackson Street. We must have been a real hindrance at times!

Stretford Road, with the Zion Institute on the right

I was nearly six when my cousin's sister-in-law Beattie asked Mam if she could take me to the Wood Street Mission, which catered for the poor families of the Manchester districts. It was nearly Christmas. Off I went with Beattie, but it seemed miles away, down Great Jackson Street to Chester Road and on to Deansgate. I did not like being at the Mission, although the people there were very nice. There was just something about the place. But when it was time to come home I was given an apple and an orange, and a small dressed doll that I treasured for a very long time.

My dad was then working at John S Bass and Company at Castlefield as a packing case maker, and Mam was working at Havelock Mill on Great Bridgewater Street; she was a tagger on the laces. Whilst they were both out at work, Grandma Jane Broster looked after my brother and me (Joseph had been born in the September of 1911).

As time passed and I was growing up, I was always minding other people's children for one reason or another. I remember I used to take a large crowd of them to Alexandra Park. We would set off with a bottle of water and some jam butties and after we had been in the park for a while, we would have a picnic. I was so young myself, it's a wonder I never lost any of them on the way there or back. If we were feeling really energetic, we would walk past Alexandra Park to the bottom of Alexandra Road, where there was an old aerodrome nicknamed the "27 steps". It was another day out, but it was a much longer walk and we only went there when we were feeling lively.

Another Christmas, when I was about eight, some people came

to our house from the Zion Institute on Stretford Road. (The building is still there, now enclosed within the Charles Barry/John Nash complex of flats and maisonettes.) These visitors used to go round all the streets, inquiring at each home if the people had any children; if so, they would be given a ticket to go to the Zion on Christmas morning. It's surprising when you're little what can excite you. Christmas morning dawned and at breakfast time all the children would make their way to the Zion. There they would be given a meat pie, one apple and orange and a cup of coffee. What a breakfast! But to some children I knew it was a feast. I remember I was very sick outside the Zion in Mulberry Street after I had drunk the coffee; even now it does not agree with me.

Nearly all the houses in Hulme were two-up, two-down and of very similar design. If you had a lobby (hall) you were posh; in some of the houses as you stepped in from the street, you were in the parlour. On practically every street corner stood a public house, some of which would not allow women in. Even they looked the same, and most of them had sawdust covering the floor and spittoons in the corners.

During the First World War the White Lion Hotel on the corner of our street was run by Mr and Mrs Kingham. They had two sons and a daughter and my cousins and I used to play with them. Molly, the daughter, was slightly crippled and unable to play outside, so I used to go into the pub to play with her; she was a lovely girl. Some nights I would be able to sleep at the pub, and this I really loved.

The time came when the family left the White Lion to take over the George on Clowes Street,

Uncle John

West Gorton, but my cousins and I were still invited and then we would be allowed to stay for up to two weeks at a time. Much as I loved my home and family, it was a sort of adventure staying in somebody else's house. Sadly, the Kinghams left the licensing business and moved into a private house in Radcliffe. We continued to visit and stay, however. Mam's sister, Aunt Ada, was a cleaner at the White Lion in those days and long after the Kinghams left, if I had been staying with Molly and it was time to return home, Aunt Ada's son Thomas would take my place, for he played with Molly's brothers. As the years passed we lost touch with the family, but I often thought about Molly and wondered what had happened to her.

Mam and Dad never went out without us; when we did go out, it was as a family. Saturday night was our favourite, when Mam and Dad, my brother Joe and I used to go to the Kings Hall Picture House on City Road, on the corner of Owen Street. It was a big building, taken over by the Brooke Bond Tea Co in later years, and as you went through the doors there was a large flight of stone steps which led up to where the picture was being shown. If we went to the first house pictures, about 6.00pm, it would still be light when we came out in the summer months. So we would all walk down City Road to Medlock Street, then along Medlock Street to Stretford Road end. There the barrow boys had their stalls. It was amazing!

One of the few open spaces in Hulme - a disused graveyard, covered over and used as a children's playground in 1913

You could buy anything you wanted and as the night grew on, things would go cheaper and cheaper. The men would show pieces of meat, shouting, "Who'll give me 2s (10p) for this?" There were vegetables, cakes, cooked black puddings and ordinary grocery items, all much cheaper than usual. Joe and I always got chocolate from my dad; that was the best part of our evening!

Because money was so short in those days, children did a lot to help out. I used to clean the neighbours' front steps, and some who took a pride in their homes had me doing the back steps, which were in the entry. Some people preferred white stone, some brown. I took great pride in this job, soaking the steps first with water, then rubbing in the stone and finishing off by smoothing the stone over. Sometimes, before it had dried, people would have walked over my cleaning, leaving their footprints behind. But week after week I lovingly did all those steps. For this I earned 2d ($\frac{1}{2}$p), which went into a box at home to help buy shoes for us all. Some people did not even pay the 2d and I would be given a jam butty as payment instead - jam was another thing I soon got to dislike!

The Great War and Afterwards

Playing in the streets, where women used to gossip on their doorsteps, we picked up quite a lot of information. I remember listening to a conversation one day and when I came home I asked my mam what "War" was. Very quietly, but firmly, she told me it did not concern me. As the weeks passed it was the main topic of conversation between the neighbours and in all the corner shops. Then it started. My dad was then only 29 and he would eventually have to go into the army. Mam always seemed to be upset, but I could not understand why. What was it, war, I kept asking myself, and why had my dad to go away?

No wonder Mam was worried! Dad told me many years later that approximately 2$\frac{1}{2}$ million men volunteered to fight in the First World War. Britain and her Allies were fighting the Germans along the River Somme in France, where Dad had been. On the first day of that battle, it was said that more than 50,000 men had been killed or injured. Even before then, as news of casualties came home, there was pressure on the government to make military service compulsory. First the single men, then the married men were "called up". Apparently there were many labelled "conscientious objectors" who were dealt with by the courts. Apart from Dad going into the army, Mam's brother, Uncle John, had also been called up. He was ten years Mam's senior but they were very close. Uncle John was a very quiet man, but a well made and handsome one.

Dad went to France and fought at Ypres (I learned later). There were some letters home, and a couple of times he got some leave. Mam used to read the letters to Joe and I; quite often I would find her reading them to herself when I came in, then she would hurriedly push them into her pinny pocket. Uncle John came home before the war had ended; he had been wounded. Apparently mustard gas was being used in France and this also had affected Uncle John, so he was discharged.

On the corner of Leinster Street and Great Jackson Street (across from the police station) a couple from Swinton ran the Tramway Inn and the woman's sister came to help in the pub. As the months passed, Uncle John used to go in the Tramway for a drink and he and the licensee's sister-in-law, who was called Eliza, started walking out together. Uncle John was 42 years old.

As the war dragged on, families were issued with food cards and you could then only get your food from a certain shop - that is, when the food was available. When you had had your groceries, the shopkeeper would cross them off your card. Several times during the war years Joe and I had to sleep at Grandma Jane Broster's at No.4. I am not sure why this was; perhaps Mam was working. Grandma Jane Broster was at one end of the big bed, Joe and I at the bottom and we used to love it.

Towards the end of the war, I can remember Grandma Jane Broster waking me up and telling me to go to the White Lion at the corner, where Aunt Ada worked. I was told, "Bring your aunt Ada at once. Tell her your Mam's ill." This I did and lo and behold, a few hours later I had a baby sister called Edna May! I had never realised there was to be a new baby, as that sort of thing was never spoken about.

Dad came home late in 1918, suffering from the effects of the mustard gas. It was the first time he had seen Edna. Mam said many a time afterwards that he would never be the same as he was before the war had started. He was discharged with £29.6.2d and two medals for fighting for King and Country, as were thousands of other men from the infantry. What an amount to be paid when eventually he had to pay with his life! It all seemed so pointless. My son now has my dad's medals and discharge papers. Dad spoke very little of life in France during the time he was there, but I can remember him telling of how the Germans used to throw gas bombs into the dugouts where the English soldiers were. These dugouts were packed too tightly and many men were killed; even the survivors had often been in the middle of two

The Tramway Inn in 1912

dead men. Dad also used to tease Mam over some little French girl called Helen, to which Mam would reply, "Oh, be off, Joe!"

As men came home from the war, their families and the neighbours would dress the street up. Anything spare was used, streamers across the street, ribbons or coloured lanterns over the doorways to their houses. It was lovely for some families, but sad for others.

Mam used to think Uncle John would never marry, but he proved her wrong. On 21st September 1918 he and Miss Eliza Rushton were married at St Michael's Church. They got a little house on Kingston Street, and according to Mam they were very happy despite the 21 years age difference between them. Their first son was born in 1919 and in 1921 Aunt Eliza gave birth to a second son. Grandma Jane Broster still worried about Uncle John even now. She used to say to Mam, "He'll never come to anything." She had some funny sayings, but they used to ring true, Mam said.

Dad had returned to John S Bass, but he was only working three days a week, trade was so bad. Eventually this led to working a week and playing a week (this meant no work that week, so no pay) and he ended up working a week and off for three. I was ten, Joe was four and Edna only a baby and times were hard. To make ends meet, Mam took in washing. For 2s (10p) a week, she used to wash for Mr Walter Hill, the grocer on George Street, who always wore white aprons and shirts at his work. Mam would put a huge pan on the fire to boil the clothes in. They would then be scrubbed in a peggy tub and last but not least, ironed on the table with a flat iron, which had to be heated on the open fire. There was no cover on the iron, but eventually Mam turned out the clothes snow white.

Life was getting back to normal after the war and there were now several places we children could go to. I started going to the York picture house on York Street (now the Aaben Cinetheque) which was then a Mission Hall. On a Monday evening they used to have what was called a Cake Hour. Mr Appleton would tell us a story from the Bible for an hour and when it was time to go home, all the children were given a piece of cake. On special days, for very good behaviour, the girls would be given a handkerchief and the boys a pen. Everybody was very happy when it was a "Special Day"! One Whit Week the people who ran the Mission and their children all walked to another Mission Hall on Greenheys Lane. As I have already said, we children would follow anything that moved, and off we went. There was no going home first to tell our parents – we just followed! None of us had a clue where we were, so we all had to wait outside the Mission Hall until we saw somebody we knew, to ask them the way home. What a to-do met us! All our mothers had been searching for us, and what a telling off we all got! Still, it didn't stop us.

At school, we were told we were being taken to Platt Fields to see the Prince of Wales on his visit to Manchester. We seemed

Joseph Hopkinson about 1916

to have been there for hours before he arrived. There were crowds and crowds of people, but I was luckier than most, right at the front. Had I just reached out, I could have touched his sleeve as he passed – I was that close. He was every young girl's dream, such a good-looking man and in later years so considerate to his people.

In 1919 an influenza outbreak hit Hulme, in fact it affected people all over the country and even some who lived abroad. They were dying like flies. Every day you would hear of somebody else you had known. Perhaps the long years of war had something to do with this epidemic. Luckily all my family escaped, but Mr Jackson, who had a dental practice on Great Jackson Street, died, followed not long afterwards by his wife. This outbreak killed off a lot more people than consumption (TB) in the short time it had hit Hulme.

Mirth and Mourning

Although these were hard times, every so often things would happen to make you laugh. For instance, there was no bathroom in our house. We used to have a huge tin bath which hung in the yard when not in use and on bath night it was brought inside and placed in front of the fire in the kitchen. One night Joe was in the bath when suddenly there was an almighty bang – the chimney had collapsed! Soot, bits of brick and all sorts of stuff came down the chimney and the smoke was everywhere. Poor Joe! There he was, still in the bath with only the white of his eyes showing. How we laughed! Mam informed Hartleys, the landlords, and they sent two men to repair the chimney, but it proved a costly exercise. At

George Street. Mr Hill's grocer's shop is on the right

the time Mam had a beautiful clock on the mantelpiece, with a front which opened to reveal two little drawers under the pendulum. Mam had very little jewellery – she did not believe in buying rubbish – so what precious little pieces of value she had were kept in the clock drawer. The two men completed their work and the chimney was fine. But after some weeks had passed, Mam had reason to open the clock for something, only to find her little pieces of treasure had all gone. She informed Hartleys, but as she had no definite proof, little could be done. Very few people had home insurance in those days.

Another comical incident was when my cousin Eric (son of Aunt Alice Jemima, Mam's older sister) had come to visit us. We were all in the parlour and Eric was sitting in the rocking chair. Faster and faster he rocked, until all at once the chair tipped over, his foot caught the table in front of the window and the plant on it went straight through the glass. Some children in the street called out, "Quick! A fight in Number Twelve!" and they all gathered round. We were never hit, but we all received a good telling off.

City Road School opened a play centre each weekday evening and nearly all the local children used to attend. If you arrived there late, you would not get in and as this happened most nights, my friends and I would just play in the playground or sit on the window sills and watch what was happening inside. My visits there stopped after a nasty incident in the playground; children can be very cruel. There was a lad called Charlie Healey, tall for his age but very slim, who came from a large family living near City Road. He had an awful squint in his eyes and everyone seemed to pick on him. The children used to chant whenever they saw him, "Skenning Ben! Skenning Ben!" One night I was sitting on the window sill by myself, watching the antics going on inside the play centre, when Charlie appeared. Of course the children in the playground started: "Skenning Ben!" they chanted. Whether because I was the nearest and had looked over when I heard the children, I don't know, but Charlie came running across to me, got hold of my ankles and dragged me off the window sill. I crashed on to the playground surface, banging my head. I think I saw stars! A passing woman shouted, Charlie ran off and she sat me up. Two brothers I knew called Ernie and Jackie Kennerley carried me home. I

Sister Edna and Cousin Mary (Ada's youngest, born December 1928) in Howard Street

had a lump like a duck egg on my head and I never went to play centre again.

One day I was sitting on the doorstep with my baby sister Edna on my knee, when suddenly all hell seemed to have broken loose! Edna was whipped off me and rushed to Old Doctor

Across the rooftops. St Wilfrid's Church is in the middle distance, centre; City Road School on the left and the York Cinema on the right

Burke's surgery. The sun that day had been very strong and she had got sunstroke. Years after, she would get pains in her head and she used to shout, "The nazes are coming! The nazes are coming!" Goodness knows what people thought, but she meant the pain was starting. I always felt it was my fault.

1920 brought the arrival of my second brother called John Henry, a lovely baby; as he grew he would always have a smile for everyone. As Mam had to go back to work, looking after John Henry was down to me. Dad or Grandma Jane Broster had him during school hours, then when I came home I took over. He was always a pleasure, such a pleasant little boy. Mam was working hard, because Dad was not earning so much. She would no sooner get home than somebody would come to say such and such a person had died, and would Mam do the necessary. The jobs she took on! Dad was a very mild-tempered man but I can recall that this always angered him. But Mam, being Mam, would never refuse anybody.

At the bottom of Howard Street, where it met Clopton Street, there was a little grocer's shop and one day in 1921 a woman came running to our house to tell Mam and Dad that Grandma Jane Broster had collapsed in the shop. Somehow, between them, Mam and Dad managed to get Grandma Jane Broster to our house and Old Doctor Burke was sent for. After he had examined her, he told Mam and Dad that Grandma Jane Broster was suffering from pneumonia and pleurisy. Sadly, she never recovered from this illness and was laid to rest at Weaste Cemetery, Salford, where Grandad Thomas was buried. Apart from her own children, she then had a total of 34 grandchildren and many friends; everyone did her proud. Grandma Jane Broster was little in height and stout, with greying hair taken back into a bun at the nape of her neck, and wherever she went, she always wore a shawl. A good woman, whom I loved and respected. Before she died, I remember Grandma Jane Broster saying to my mam, "Watch over our little John Henry. He will never make anything." We did not understand then what she meant.

I started going to Uncle John's and Aunt Eliza's house most nights after tea with John Henry, as this gave Mam and Dad a break. Uncle John's two sons, John and William, used to make a right fuss of our little John Henry and like any baby, he would chuckle away for them. We were always made very welcome. Sadly, Uncle John's health wasn't very good, which limited him in what he could do. Mam blamed the war and told me Grandma Jane Broster had confided in her just weeks before she had died that she would only give Uncle John another couple of years.

As time went on, my dad's health was not improving either. He had started with heart trouble now and Mam was working all the hours God sent to support us.

As if that wasn't enough, at the beginning of 1922 little John Henry started to be poorly. Old Doctor Burke tried everything, but when all else had failed, little John Henry was ordered into Booth Hall Hospital. There they diagnosed him as having a gastric stomach. Dad was ill with pneumonia and pleurisy at the time, so Mam, on top of everything else she had to do, was up and down to Booth Hall every day. It was quite a journey. The trams in those days only went as far as Charlestown Road, and anybody who has been to Booth Hall will know how long this road is. I used to go with Mam but I was not allowed in, because I was not yet fourteen (the legal limit when someone was very poorly). I was 13 years, 11 months. Me, who had had to look after John Henry since he was born because of Mam working! Me, who had taken him everywhere I had gone! I was heartbroken.

On 24th April 1922 Mam had gone to see John Henry and she was told he had taken a turn for the worse and if Dad was to see him alive again, she had better go and bring him. How on earth Mam did it, I don't know, but she did. She rushed home and got Dad out of bed in the parlour (the stairs had proved too much for him these past few months and he now slept down there). Dad saw little John Henry for the last time and later that night John Henry passed away. I was fourteen on 1st May. Another funeral at Weaste. He was laid to rest near Grandma Jane Broster and her words now came back to us. It seemed to me all my loved ones were being taken away from me and Mam and Dad were devastated.

But life had to go on and sticking to the weekly routine helped. As far back as I can remember, Mam always baked every Sunday and considering that all the cooking was done on an open fire, everything would be perfect. By Sunday tea-time the dresser would be piled up from end to end with pies, custards, fatty cakes and currant cakes. A load would be sent to Aunt Ada's and the smell would travel from one end of the street to the other, so that neighbours would come on the pretext of borrowing something and would end up going away with a pie or a custard.

In the week Mam made "tater 'ash". One neighbour in particular always came in at the right time and ended up having a pan of "tater 'ash" on a regular basis. We think it was the only decent meal her family got in a week. Dad's likes were few, but one favourite of his was Cambridge sausage. There were only two

Corner of Upper Jackson Street and Warde Street

shops in Hulme that sold them, one on City Road and the other on Upper Jackson Street near to Warde Street. Woe betide me if I went to another shop! He could always tell.

Starting Work

At school I had passed the scholarship to go to Ducie Avenue High School. I was very proud and happy, but alas it was not to be. Owing to the circumstances at home, I had to leave school.

Our school board man was called Mr Walton and he was the one who helped us. In order for me to start work I had to get a copy of the Factory and Workshop Act 1901, which stated my name, age and so on. Because Dad was earning next to nothing and in poor health, Mr Walton arranged everything so that I was able to leave school before the end of term. I was in school one day and in work the next.

An acquaintance of Mam's who was known to everyone as "Aunty Melia" got me my first, and really my only, job at Barlows Limited on Chepstow Street in Manchester city centre. I took this as seriously as I did my schooldays and once I had got over the disappointment of having to leave school, I really loved going to work. The cotton trade at this time was very very busy and they were working what was called "double shifts". As fast as one person finished their hours, somebody else took over the job, such was the workload.

Barlows' four storey building stood on the corner of Chepstow

The Peveril of the Peak in the 1950s

Street and Great Bridgewater Street. Barlows owned the whole building but it was divided up inside into numbers 16, 18 and 20 and several other firms had premises there. The chief occupants of No.20 were Jacob Behrens & Sons; No.18 was known as Chepstow House and housed Sydney Hudson, among others; no.16, where I started work, was known as Calcutta House.

The main entrance was on Chepstow Street, from where a flight of stone steps led up to the swing doors, where the lift was. We were not allowed to use that entrance, though. We had to go through the huge wrought iron gates of what was known as "No.16 hovel" and walk up the stairs. In the early years No.16 was where the horses and carts came to deliver or collect goods; later, of course, they were replaced by

lorries and vans. The stairs from No.16 were very dark, but half way up there was a small window from which you could see the canal banks and the woodworks called Smith, Wilson and Batty, then further back still were Mosley Street and Central Station. On the first floor, offices ran the length of Barlows building. The second floor was the warehouse and the top floor was the making-up room. A cellar also ran the length of the building.

This was to become my kingdom, so to speak. When I first started at Barlows, where Great Bridgewater Street met Mosley Street there was a row of shops. They consisted of The Hut, which sold newspapers, toffees and cigarettes, then Ellen's - she sold pies and cakes - then came Campbell's, a cook shop; you could stay and eat in there or buy something and take it away. All these shops in later years were pulled down to make way for Mosley Street bus station.

On the other side of Bridgewater Street stood the pub called the Britons Protection, then Warde's cafe and a store where one could buy anything for horses, including their food. Horses were used a lot in the warehouse business. Next to this stood a textile warehouse and a sewing factory, then Havelock Mill (where Mam had worked), a printer's premises and a private house. Tootal Broadhurst occupied the rest of Bridgewater Street right up to Oxford Road.

Across from Barlows on Chepstow Street stood another pub, this one called the Peveril of the Peak, and quite a few of the buildings after that were in the textile trade. Many fine buildings occupied Chepstow Street. Glazebrook, Steel and Co Textiles was one, and another

City Road from the corner of Crown Street, looking towards Great Jackson Street, in 1954. The tall building is the Victoria Hotel; Dr Burke's surgery was next door to the right

warehouse was used by the Salvation Army. Next to the "Sally Army" was a pair of huge iron gates which led through to Oxford Street; Booth and Others Ltd, another textile warehouse, occupied the space between Chepstow Street and Oxford Street.

Along Oxford Street were Lyons Cafe, the Oxford Picture House, the photographer's called Guttenberg's, then a really posh sweet shop and the Manchester Hippodrome. Back down on Bridgewater Street, next door to Smith, Wilson and Batty's woodworks, was a basement shop where I had to take all the workers' knives and scissors to be sharpened. The old man there did a roaring trade with all the warehouses in Manchester.

Apart from Aunty Melia, who worked as a parceller in the cellar, Barlows had a large staff. The manager over No.16 was a Mr Entwistle, the foreman was Mr Alex Gledhill and the under-foreman was Mr Alf Holmes. There were 51 women in the making-up room, mainly hookers with a few material sorters. In addition, there were 9 male makers-up, 9 male stampers and three other men whose job was to distribute the work to the women. The three hoist men were the brothers Albert and Leslie Lea and Mr Alf Bamber. Down in the cellar the foreman was Mr George Gledhill (brother of Alex) with two male packers and a foreman packer, and six women parcelling the goods. Some of the staff belonged to the same family.

I started off as an errand girl, sweeping and cleaning, running messages and so forth. My hours were 8.00am until 6.00pm Monday to Friday and 8.00 till 1.00 on Saturdays for the grand wage of 10s (50p). The hoist man, Mr Albert Lea, was very kind to me and took me under his wing from the day I started there. Among other things, I used to go for the lunches for the men and women staff and sometimes they would give me money for doing so. Mr Lea would put this into a box at the beginning of the week, and at the end of the week he would round the money off, so that I got 6d (2½p). I was rich! Mam always let me keep whatever had been given to me, because she had my wages to help run the home.

One of the errands I had to go was for a woman at Barlows who several times sent me to a chemist's shop on Liverpool Road near Deansgate. I didn't really like this woman but I was too scared to say anything to her. She was very abrupt - just used to give me a note and say it was for some special pills, always adding, "You must not tell anybody what you are going for." Being so scared of her, I promised I never would. Time passed and one day the chemist must have been a little suspicious. He asked me who the pills were for, then if I had ever taken any of them. More questions followed - it was a real inquisition. I told him I never even opened the packet, that I just gave it to the woman concerned. Somehow or other, there were words at work between the foreman and this woman and I never had to go to the chemist's again, but she used to give me some terrible looks whenever I crossed her path. Had I known then what I learned much later, I would never have gone on this errand.

I had a much nicer task to do for one of the men at Barlows, and this was to book seats at the Opera House for him and his wife. I used to dream of how grand it would be to go there; even now I have never been inside!

As well as running errands, I had to brew up and clean when necessary. If there was nothing for me to do, which was very rare, I used to go and watch the hookers, the people who hooked the cloth. Two girls worked with one maker-up. The material would come in as, say, 36" widths and be placed in bundles on the floor near the hooking frame. A corner of the material would be put on one hook and the other corner on the opposite hook, and this was done continually until the allotted yardage was reached. Then the material would be taken off the frame, doubled and placed on the floor. The goods would be sorted into the various designs, then put on a truck. The stamper would come and stamp them and eventually they went to the cellar to be parcelled and made into bales. As my working life progressed, I too went on to learn how to hook the cloth.

The majority of the staff were of my parents' ages, but there were a few younger ones. Three in particular I really liked were Rosie May, Beattie Ackerley and Elsie Smith. Most Thursday nights Elsie and I would go to the pictures; she would pay one week, then I would pay the next. We went mainly to the Gaiety or the Tivoli on Peter Street or the Futurist on Great Ducie Street. Elsie's young man had emigrated to Australia and she was saving up to go and join him; a couple of years later, off she went.

On Saturday afternoons, providing all the work at home was done, I would go to the Penny Bazaar on Stretford Road. Before I went to spend my money, I would walk to the outside of Barlows' building and stand looking up at it - I was so proud to be working there. The Penny Bazaar was where Marks and Spencer first started and in those days a 6d (2½p) went a long way. There were books, sweets and toys and I never knew what to buy - they were happy times. As I loved reading, I normally ended up with a book and I

Some of the girls on one of Barlow's picnics. Mary Jordan is in the middle of the back row. Third from left, front row, is Rosie May (now Lyons), and sixth from left is Elsie Smith (now Lowe)

soon started buying the weekly magazines, all only 2d then. The popular ones were "Betty's Paper", "Poppy", "Weekend Novel", "Red Star", "Red Letter", "Golden Star", "My Weekly", "Weekly Welcome", "Pam's Paper" and "Picture Show". I would read for hours in bed with only the candle for a light - that is, until Dad cottoned on to what I was doing and told me I would go cross-eyed!

A yearly picnic for the workers was arranged at Barlows and in my first year there they decided to go to Bakewell and Matlock Bath. Mam and Dad had said I could go. The big day dawned and off we went in a coach, stopping first at a public house before we reached Bakewell. Because I was so young I could not go in and the coach driver bought me a lemonade. The time passed and he brought me another, but when he asked if I wanted a third lemonade I refused, saying I could not go home drunk. Goodness knows what he thought of me, but he did laugh! It was a lovely day out.

For the following year's picnic we all went to the beautiful city of Chester. As usual on the way there the coach stopped several times at the various pubs and on arrival at Chester everyone went into a pub on City Road, the name of which escapes me. Beattie Ackerley and I went up and down the streets, looking in all the shops. We must have walked miles that day, but I think we were the only ones to look round this charming place! I bought a small tortoiseshell sugar bowl and a matching fruit dish for my mam which

Demolition in the Medlock district near the rubber works in 1925

are still going strong today. After a while Beattie and I were tired and instead of waiting for the coach to leave, we caught the train home.

Into the Twenties

Somehow, living in Hulme, you were used to its smell; it was part and parcel of life and you became unaware of it: the coke steaming away at the gasworks and the stench of rubber from the Macintosh (Dunlops) blew all over Hulme. Dad used to say before he would let me work at the Mac, he would see me unemployed. Rumour had it that

the people who worked there suffered with their chests; it was even implied that it caused TB. You could tell by the person's clothes where they worked, for the smell of the Mac used to cling to them like a second skin. All the little streets from Hulme Street to Newcastle Street and down to Cambridge Street were permanently covered with a white powder which came from the huge chimneys. Lord only knows what it did to the people who worked there day after day!

In 1924 there was a General Election. Being so young, I didn't know anything about politics, though I remember seeing the blue and red voting posters in the windows of the Co-op on Great Jackson Street a year or two later. "Vote for Allan" they said; he was one of the last Liberal candidates for Hulme in the days before Labour gained popularity. I used to listen to what Mam and Dad had to say, however, and I found out that the people involved in 1924 were Mr Stanley Baldwin for the Conservative Party, Mr Asquith for the Liberals and Mr Ramsay MacDonald for the Labour Party. Both my parents and most of the family were strong Labour people and were disappointed when the Conservatives won.

As a little girl I had always attended St Stephen's Church on City Road, going every Sunday afternoon and evening, and as I grew older I used to read the lessons at Sunday School. I had always looked forward to Whitsuntide as a child, for if the money situation wasn't too bad at home it meant two sets

Walter Davies (Liberal) canvassing in Hulme in November 1922

of new clothes. Most children got new clothes simply because it was Whitsun, but if you walked with the Church, a new set had to be bought for that purpose. On Whit Sunday the church people used to walk around the parish dressed in new but "ordinary" clothes, and Whit Monday was the big day when all the clothes had to be in white; I guess as a little girl I felt like a princess of sorts. On this day we would walk to Albert Square where all the other churches congregated and every seven years a church would be picked and invited to go into Manchester Cathedral. While I was with St Stephen's I went twice into the Cathedral, a really beautiful building. It was only after some ribbing from a girl friend that I began missing the odd Sunday at St Stephen's and eventually I stopped going completely. I felt very guilty about this, as though I was doing something really bad.

St Stephen's, City Road

The old Hulme library was next to the Town Hall on Stretford Road, an enormous place and so very very cold inside. As I loved books, I was always going there, but the two women who worked there were real tyrants. You could only take out one book at a time then, and if you had not picked one within a few minutes of going in, the women would come round and watch you. It really made you feel uncomfortable. Given the opportunity, I would have stayed in the library all day. The fine for a book returned late was 1d, but I usually took mine back in good time.

Hulme Town Hall and Library

Uncle John's health had deteriorated and he was now unable to work. Mam helped Aunt Eliza as best she could, but with Dad's health not being any better, times for us all were hard. Aunt Eliza was really struggling; she had two little boys, as I have already said, and was having another baby. When Uncle John passed away at the early age of 48, Mam was beside herself with grief, they had been so very close. Poor Uncle John! The doctor's report was that he had died through gangrene poisoning, the result of injuries sustained in the First World War. Again

Grandma Jane Broster's words had been right. He too was laid to rest at Weaste Cemetery and soon afterwards, on 5th October 1924, Aunt Eliza gave birth to a little girl. How sad that she would never know what a fine man her dad had been! Aunt Eliza stayed on in Kingston Street for many years.

I soon began to love the pictures - I must have taken after my dad! Whatever one of us saw, we would know whether or not the other would like it. The Central Picture Hall on Stretford Road, later known as the Triangle, sometimes had a woman playing the piano and a man playing the fiddle, but they were never in tune with each other. Children would be running up and down the aisles in the picture house, too - it's a good job they were silent films!

I used also to go to the "Pop" facing Upper Jackson Street, and to the Crescent, which was further down on Chapman Street. The Pop used to have "turns" on and Mr Harold Mason, who then managed the White Lion, sang there more than once. Some of my favourite silent stars then were Tom Mix, Buck Jones, Mary Pickford, the Costellos and the Barrymores. One night I had been to the Pop with a friend called Lizzie and when we were coming home we got into conversation with two boys we had seen before at the pictures, but had only nodded to until then. One was called John Turner, and from that evening onward, he and I started walking out together.

Around the Christmas time the

front of our house started bulging and once more Mam got in touch with Hartleys. In due course, they sent some men to do the repairs, and one of the workmen always seemed to be coming through the house. Our Joe was being particularly awkward for Dad on one of these occasions and Dad was reading him the riot act. The man stopped and told Dad not to shout at Joe. Dad was a very quiet man, but he became angry at this and told him so in no uncertain terms: "Mind your own bloody business and stop coming through this house," he said. "I know your game!" We had all been thinking the workman was going to the toilet in the yard, when in fact he had been going straight through the yard and up to the pub at the corner, then back again. It's a wonder we got the repairs done!

Joe was a good lad at heart but always seemed to be where he shouldn't. For instance, if Dad said he was to be in at eight, Joe would always arrive at five past! One day Dad wanted Joe, so I was sent to find him. I went to all the usual places but did not see him anywhere, and soon quite a few of the neighbours joined in the search. Someone said he had been seen at Castlefield Wharf and a friend of mine called Lily Thompson said she would go down there with me. The bridge used to swing in those days and all I could see was the dark water swirling about; I was terrified but mesmerised by it at the same time. After what seemed an eternity, a lad shouted that Joe had arrived home. When all came to all, he had not been anywhere near Castlefield. I was so glad to see him I could have cried from sheer relief!

He was always getting into scrapes. He and his mates used to go to All Saints Park to play in the days when the church stood in the middle of the park (it was hit in the blitz and later pulled down). One day our Joe, being nosey, found the door of the burial vault unlocked and went down to have a look. His mates promptly locked the door and he was in there for quite a few minutes before they let him out. He never said why he was so frightened, but he never went to the park again.

In 1926, when he was 14, Joe left school and started work. His first job was as an errand boy for Maurice Edwards on Oldham Street, Manchester, taking goods here, there and everywhere with only a push-bike to help. On one occasion

he was taking a parcel from the town centre to a shop on Bury Old Road for his boss. The parcel was too large for Joe's bike so he had to catch a tram and when Joe reached his stop a car hit him and then drove off, not bothering to see if he was hurt or not. Joe was taken to Booth Hall Hospital with a broken leg. He was in for some time and Booth Hall became another hospital I visited regularly. But what an ordeal for my parents, having to go again to the place where little John Henry had died! We learnt much later that the driver of the car was a well known Salford MP and Mam and Dad were advised to go and see a Poor Man's Lawyer. The offices of the Poor Law Guardians were opposite All Saints Park on the corner of Stretford Road and they went there to see if they could claim for Joe's loss of wages while he was in hospital. Dad first had to pay out £5 to the lawyer (a fortune in those days) and when the case was eventually heard in court, Mam and Dad were awarded £3 to cover Joe's wages. Justice! I ask you!

When I was eighteen I learnt how to sort the goods at Barlows into eight or ten piece bundles. A man then used to stamp the bundles and pile them on a truck about four layers high, putting a steel plate on top to hold them down and flatten them. Then the truck would be sent down to the cellar to go into a press, which made the bundles flatter and smaller. A woman working in the cellar then put them into bales and they would be sent off by horse and cart to the

docks, from where they would be dispatched to destinations all over the world.

Outside work, I was having fun. During the 1920s the waltz, which had been the "in" dance, was replaced by the Shimmy-shake, the Black Bottom and the Charleston. Older people thought these dances were immoral (what would they think of today's?). Fashion had changed also and the girls were wearing "flapper dresses" with skirts above the knee – very daring! Hair styles too had taken on a new look and hair was cut very short, bobbed and then shingled.

Talking pictures started about that time, mainly musicals at first. The earliest one I saw was "The Perfect Alibi" at the La Scala on Oxford Road, and I have never forgotten seeing Al Jolson sing 'Sonny Boy' in "The Singing Fool" – that was a wonderful film. Layton and Johnstone were very popular then and records by Regal and Columbia cost 2s6d (12½p). Many theatrical people lived near Oxford Road in those days, in the streets off Upper Brook Street named after the months of the year – January Street, February Street and so on. The site of the Manchester Hip on Oxford Street was taken over by the Gaumont cinema, a really lovely place, and later there were some wonderful live shows in the theatre at Ardwick Green. The Theatre Royal, Gaiety and Manchester Palace were other favourites of mine.

When Edna was about ten, she decided she wanted her hair cutting, so she sat on a three-legged stool out in the back

Upper Jackson Street School and the Popular Cinema in the 1950s

yard and I started the job. She would not sit still, turning one way, then the other. Every time I looked at her from the front, one side would be longer than the other, so I would snip a bit more off. It ended up a complete disaster! In the end my young man, John, had the task of trying to neaten it off and he was so good at it that he got the job permanently. Edna would not let me near her ever again!

As my 21st birthday approached I cleaned in my spare time at a shop on Great Jackson Street run by Mrs Martha Parsons. She sold sweets, cigarettes and papers. Sometimes I was allowed to serve the customers, and this really delighted me, for I used to think when I was older I would like a shop of my own. I loved working at Mrs Parsons'. The shop had a big window in which she used to display toffees and chocolates. Inside, the counter was L-shaped and magazines and books would be shown in rows on the counter top. Opposite the window was a huge showcase with four glass doors, containing a display of books and toys. A wide shelf jutted out from the wall with cigarettes and tobacco on it and nearby was a smaller shelf holding the till. When money was put in the till, a bell on the top would swivel round, but if I served anybody, I used to put the money under the counter. I was terrified of that till! In fact, I used to pray people would have the right money when they came in. Mrs Parsons' husband worked for the newspapers and she had a son and a daughter; my sister Edna

Mary Jordan and fiance John

used to wheel the little girl round the streets. Sadly, the son died of meningitis.

My 21st birthday fell on a Wednesday, and considering the money situation at home I was very lucky to be having a party. Mam had booked a room in the White Lion Hotel and the invitations had been sent out. Apart from it being my 21st, it was also my engagement party to John; we had been courting since I was eighteen. 21st cards then were like today's postcards, each with a verse on, and I still treasure them now, many years on. Some of my presents were lovely! Mam and Dad bought me a gold watch on a bracelet and John bought me a beautiful engagement ring, a diamond surrounded by smaller ones, all in a diamond shape. In those days, when it was a girl's 21st, most of the presents were bought with her "bottom drawer" in mind. I received a glass dressing table set with one glass tray on to which three little bowls (for powder etc), two candlesticks and one ring tree fitted. As well as this, I was given two tea services, scarves and stockings.

Hulme Streets and Shops

The shops we had in Hulme then would have to be seen to be believed. On Great Jackson Street alone, from City Road to Stretford Road, there were more than 70, selling everything you could wish for. In the early days, Dr Eales' surgery was on one side at the City Road end, followed by three private houses. Then:

From Hamilton St to Leinster St

(Numbers are those in 1925, unless otherwise stated.)

Robinson's pram and toy shop (68)
Smolensky's new and second hand clothes' shop. They were Jewish and changed their name to Small's after the war. (70)
The Tramway beerhouse; later, this became a dentist's. (72)

From Leinster St to Howard St

Collins' fruit shop, later a grocer's. (74 in 1915)
Private house (76)
Cardus's. They made mouldings, castings and so on and I used to run errands for them and clean their steps. Later their premises became a flower shop. (78)

From Howard St to Bedford St

The White Lion Hotel (80/82)
The hay shop (84/86)

Sister Edna in Whit Week

From Bedford St to New St

Jones and Dunkley, a shoe shop and cobbler's. This later became a Co-op shop, above which was the "Good Intent" Mission. (88/90)
Shumm's pork butcher's; this family was persecuted during the First World War. (94)
Banks, the hosiery shop. (98)
Stanway's cookshop. (102 in 1915)
Yard belonging to the wholesale stationer's.
Harvey's, the cobbler's. (110)
Ogden's toffee shop. (112)
The Meadow Dairy (later a grocer's). (114)
Clapp's, the chip shop. (116)
Toffee shop. (118/120)

From New Street to Rutland St

Ross, the grocer's (124 in 1915)
Stationer's - in an emergency, the people here would make a telephone call for you (128)
Private house (132)
Jackson's, the dentist's (132 in 1915)
The doctors' Barretts' surgery (134)

The shops near Rutland Street changed hands a lot, but among them was an antique and second hand shop at one stage and on the corner was the Severn Valley Dairy grocer's. They used to have huge cheeses in the window and rumour had it that if you passed the shop late at night, you would see the mice on top of the cheeses! Needless to say, we did not shop there! A land mine fell on this corner in World War Two.

From Rutland St to Tomlinson St

The chip shop (144)

Empty shop; much later, this became a taxi firm (148)
Cake shop (150)
Newsagent's (152)
Holland's, the chemist's (156)
Printer's - this was where I got my 21st cards printed (158)
Ice cream shop (160)
Shop where they charged batteries for radios (162)

Entry leading to Brunswick St

Bedding maker's (164)
Herbalist's (166)
Pet food shop (168)
Mrs Thomas's shop for ladies' underwear etc (172)
Boot mender's (174)
Newsagent's (178)
Holy shop selling Bibles and statues (182)
Toffee shop (188)
Glazier's (190/192)

From Tomlinson St to Stretford Rd

Optician's (194)
Fishing tackle shop (198)
Deakin's cigarette's and cigars (this was 190 Stretford Rd)

Now for the opposite side, coming down:

From City Rd to Park Place

Miss Webb's (87 City Rd)
Madam Bergin's hat shop (91 Gt Jackson St)
Cusick's furniture shop (93)

The Fire and Police Station was down Park Place.

From Park Place to George St

Mellor's key shop (99)
Richards', the barber's (nicknamed "Humpy's") (101)
Martha Parsons' newspaper shop, where I worked (103)

Provisions and cake shop, run by Mrs Dunkerley (105)
Lewis's gown shop (107)
Printer's (109)
Pettener's, the butcher's (111 in 1915)
Needler's wholesale toffee factory (corner of George Street)

From George St to Chester St

The Crown public house (111a)
Madam Gochin's dress shop (113 in 1930)
Cake shop (115)
Toulmin's pawnbroker's (two shops together, selling both new and second hand clothes) (117/119)
Dressmaker's (121)
Second hand bookshop (123)
Pie shop (127)
Cigarettes and tobacco shop (131)

At this point there were hoardings running round from Great Jackson Street into Chester Street, advertising the local pictures.

From Chester St to Clarendon St

Euerby's, the butcher's (137)
Kennedy's sweet shop (139)
Tailor's (141)
Goodwin's shoe shop (two shops in one) (141/151)
Tobacconist's (153)
Fish shop (155)
Dewhirst's tailor's (159/161)
Howard's pawnshop, which later moved to Stretford Road (165)

From Clarendon St to Tomlinson St

There were a lot of shops on this stretch, but those that stand out in my memory are:

"Mick's" or "The Little Wonder".

I think his real name was Alf Goodman, but his wife always called him Mick and this was how the shop was known. They were Jewish people who sold dresses, underwear and so on, and Mick used to hang the clothes in rows, one below the other; line after line would be attached to the wall outside the shop. (167 in 1930)
Two provision shops (173/179)
Private house (181a)
A bookshop (181)
Mrs Taylor's flower shop (187)
The music shop (213)

From Tomlinson St to Stretford Rd

Flower shop (217 in 1927)
The Exchange Drapery Stores, later bought by Woolworth's (182-188 Stretford Road)

I could go on forever; the businesses continued over Stretford Road and over City Road. In the opposite direction, between Upper Chorlton Road and Cambridge Street, there was every kind of shop a person could desire. At White's on the corner of Welcomb Street and Stretford Road a really lovely top coat would cost you £4.19.11d. Lewis's was the shop for dresses, and they sold for 16s11d. Last but not least, when the Bata Shoe Company came to Hulme we were really made. Their shop was on Stretford Road. The styles then were slip-ons, ordinary flat shoes or the high-heeled ones which had straps and buckles on the side, all priced at 10s11d. "Broadway coats" were in fashion, single-breasted and slightly flared round the bottom

Great Jackson Street

with a belt which would be fastened really tightly to show off your waistline. I can remember buying a cinammon brown costume, the skirt of which had a split on the left hand side with a button fastening at the hem. The coat had a satin ribbon round the edge of the sleeves and over the top of the pocket. Frocks (nowadays called dresses) were mainly plain with V-necks and they too had belts. You could choose long or short sleeves, then Peter Pan collars came into vogue.

Aunt Ada's husband, our Uncle Tom, worked as a carter at Kendal Milne's on Deansgate. Many was the soaking he got taking their goods from place to place in all sorts of weather. One day he was unable to go to work because he was feeling ill and Aunt Ada sent for Old Doctor Burke. After examining Uncle Tom, the doctor diagnosed pneumonia and ordered him into Withington Hospital. Looking back, I think Doctor Burke sent Uncle Tom to Withington because at that time Aunt Ada was working there. She had seven children and another one on the way, and he probably thought it would make things easier for her. Unfortunately, Uncle Tom was only in Withington for three days, then he passed away. Poor Aunt Ada, and poor Mam! Another burden for her to help with.

Crown, Great Jackson Street

Aunt Ada bought a family grave at Weaste to bury Uncle Tom.

The cotton trade had started to tail off around 1929, then came the prints from Africa, Australia and New Zealand, which were a big boon to the industry. The cloth was first creased on a machine to make it half its width, down to 20, 30 or 40-yard pieces. The pieces were then made up: one woman would put two paper bands round the material, advertising what it was. Another woman would attach a card to it and write on the width, design and the yardage of the piece, then someone else would parcel it up in paper. In later years, the paper was changed to cellophane. The designs would then be sorted out and made into bales and this done, they would go down to the cellar, where they would be packed and sent on their way. It was heavy and hard work, standing up for most of the working day, but I enjoyed my job very much and met many people from all walks of life over the years.

Around the beginning of 1930 we got a new hoist man at Barlows, about whom people talked, as they always do when a new face appears. His name was William Jordan, but more about him later.

Stretford Road from Great Jackson Street, with Woolworth's on the left

The Police Station on Great Jackson Street was a very friendly place. Mam knew the name of each policeman who worked there (probably because of her knocking-up round). But then the policemen talked to everyone, in fact they knew most people by their first names. Each evening at 10.00pm they would come out of the station and all walk one behind the other in single file, until they reached the corner of Stretford Road and Great Jackson Street. There they would branch off and each would go to his own beat, trying shop doors and so on. Burglaries did happen then, but because they were so rare, when they did occur they would be talked about for weeks. There was very little violent crime, though sadly, the police did quite often have to remove bodies from the canal or the river; sometimes these were murder victims, but more often the result of accidents or suicide. I can only remember three or four major incidents from those early years.

One Bonfire Night a policeman doing his rounds came down Bedford Street near to St Wilfrid's Church. In those days the churches were open day and night and on this particular night some lads were inside the church messing about, with one acting as a lookout. On seeing the policeman, this lad must have panicked and thought he was going to the church. In their rush to get away, one of them threw a squib, obviously without looking where it was going. Unfortunately it exploded in the policeman's face and he lost an eye. I don't think this was intentional; they were probably scared at being caught in the church.

Our local grocery shop on Bedford Street belonged to Mr and Mrs Hesketh; their four sons later took over the business and ran it until it closed in the 1960s as a result of the slum clearance. Apart from vegetables, you could buy practically anything you required from them. One of their sons, Freddie, was drowned at Mark Addy's Bridge and shortly after this tragedy another was to happen to Mrs Martha Parsons, who ran the newsagent's where I had worked some years earlier. Her mother, Mrs Barlow, was also found drowned in Mark Addy's water.

Just after Bill Jordan started at Barlows a young woman's body was found at Red Bank. Murder seemed to happen less often in those days and it really did cause a stir. Eventually the police caught the man who had killed this woman; his home address was on Medlock Street, Hulme, opposite the gasworks. When the case was published in the papers, can you imagine the talk that went around Barlows' building? The man found guilty of the murder was a William Jordan! I'm happy to say there was no connection; only the names were the same.

Into the 1930s

John and I were still courting; no marriage date yet. His life too had been hard. His mother had died when he was a little boy, and he and his brothers and sisters had been put into care until his father remarried. Then, all together again, they lived at Walters Place, at the corner of Hyde Street and Moss Lane. John worked at Metrovicks on permanent nights, so I only saw him at weekends when he wasn't working. Even then I wasn't sure. Every Monday his step-mother had to pawn his suit, getting it back out on a Friday, and if there was not enough money, his suit had to stay at the shop. John would never come out at weekends if he didn't have his suit.

In the 1930s the Co-op shop again had the voting posters up. The Labour movement was now gaining strength and their man was a Mr McElwee, who was supported by Barbara Castle. The Conservative chap, Colonel Sir Joseph Nall, owned a carrier firm. At election time, rumour had it that if one of his employees was found not to have voted for him, they got the sack. I never knew if there was any truth in this rumour, or how he would have found out how they had voted in the first place – I thought the vote was a private thing.

Edna was growing up. She was always borrowing something or other of mine, mainly make up – I used Icilma face cream and scent in those days. One morning she was there in front of the mirror (she couldn't walk past a mirror without stopping) when Dad came into the room. In his sternest voice (he never shouted) he told her to go and wash the make up off. Mind you, she was still only going to school. Soon afterwards she reached her fourteenth birthday and left school to start work.

A woman who lived at the bottom of Howard Street got Edna her first job, learning how to become a machinist at Haworth's mill on Ordsall Lane, Salford, but in order to get to work Edna had to cross Mark Addy's Bridge. Unemployment was high in those days and there were always men on the bridge, possibly only passing the time of day with each other or perhaps hoping to hear early news of a job. Still, there were all these men. Being only 14, Edna was very quiet and she became quite nervous about having to pass these men. One night she voiced her fears at home. Dad immediately said to Mam, "She doesn't go there any more," and the next morning he went with her to work and waited while she told them she had to finish working there. Dad insisted that Edna ask for a reference in order to go for another job. The company were quite reluctant to

St Wilfrid's Church in later years

give her one, as she had only worked there for two and a half weeks, but when Edna mentioned that her dad was outside, they did produce one. Fortunately she got another job quickly, again sewing, and she enjoyed it; this firm was called Bowlings on the Hulme/Salford border down Egerton Street.

Dad's health had really gone worse. The doctor never seemed to be away and the bills for all Dad's medicines were very high, but that didn't matter – Mam would have found the money from somewhere. Sadly, in the October of 1933 he passed away, aged only 48 years. Truthfully he had suffered on and off with one thing and another ever since he had come back from the First World War. He was a good, kind man, a loving and much loved husband and a devoted father; everyone spoke well of him. Dad was laid to rest at Weaste Cemetery like so many of the Jones family before him. There were several horse-drawn carriages at the funeral and neighbours said afterwards it was fit for a king. Aunt Eliza, despite all the troubles she had, bought a beautiful wreath for Dad; everybody, I thought, had had more than their share of death. A few weeks after Dad had died, the Minister came to see Mam, and I have never forgotten what he said. He told her she had been silly to waste so much money on a funeral for Dad, when she had a family to support. Mam, still very upset over losing Dad,

Mary Jordan in May 1931

replied, "It was the last thing I could do for Joe, and he was well worth it." With that, the Minister left. Mam continued to live at No.12 Howard Street for many years.

Yet another tragedy was soon to come home to us. Mam's sister, our Aunt Ada, had always lived with Grandma Jane Broster and she and Uncle Tom took over the house after Grandma died. As they lived so near, we were very close. As I have said, Uncle Tom died in the August of 1928, too soon to see the baby girl who was born in the December, the youngest of their five sons and three daughters. The middle daughter, Edna, was now a bonny girl of 13. In Barlows building, where I worked, a firm had opened from whom you could buy material at wholesale prices. I bought two designs and had dresses made up, but one would not fit me, so I had given it to my cousin Edna. At tea time on Friday, 17th November 1933, a friend had called for Edna to go with her to the play centre. Edna was wearing the dress I had given her and was looking into the mirror on the mantelpiece when the outside door opened. The draught blew the skirt of her dress over the fireguard and it caught fire. Edna was very badly burned and was rushed to the Manchester Royal Infirmary; I went with her because Aunt Ada was out at work at the time this happened.

On the Saturday afternoon, I went to the hospital again and whilst I was there a doctor came up and asked me to go and get Aunt Ada, as there was nothing else they could do for Edna and time was running out. If anyone reading this has been into the Manchester Royal Infirmary, they will understand what I mean by my next statement. There are miles and miles of corridors. I remember running from the ward, down corridor after corridor until I reached the lodge, where I asked the porter on duty to telephone through to Jackson Street Police Station and get a message to Aunt Ada's house. Thank God, Aunt Ada did get to the hospital in time. Young Edna died at 6.00pm; she had only gone the clock round. It seemed there was to be no end to our family's grief.

At the beginning of 1934, a heavy fog covered Hulme and all of Manchester. In Piccadilly you literally couldn't see a hand in front of you. It lasted a couple of days and made a lot of people very ill, especially those who had chest problems.

Time was passing and somehow

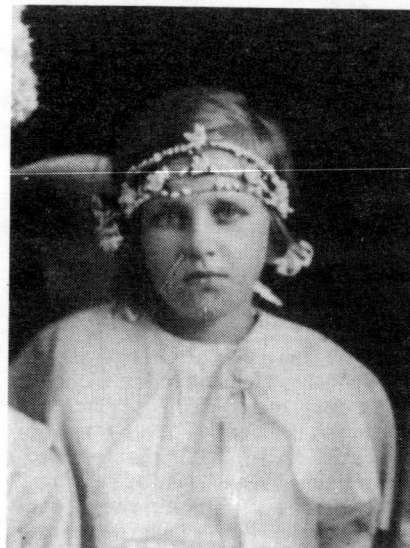

Cousin Edna at Whit Week

my engagement to John came to an end; we didn't have any rows but we just seemed to drift apart. At work I got to know Bill Jordan, whose wife had died from pernicious anaemia, leaving him with a baby son, also called William. From being a baby, Bill junior was a very sickly child, in and out of Booth Hall Hospital and this was the beginning of my courting days, visiting hospitals. When not in hospital, young Bill and his dad lived with Bill's mother at 93 Abbott Street, Collyhurst. Bill's father Patrick had died in 1929, but also living at home was Bill's younger brother Lawrence. The family had originally come from Blackburn in 1912 because of Bill's father's job with the gas board, though I believe his mother Catherine originated from the Liverpool area and his father had Irish ancestry.

Of the four children – Thomas, Bill, Annie and Lawrence – Bill was the first to come to Manchester with his dad; the rest of the family joined them once they had obtained accommodation. They belonged to St Patrick's Church on Livesey Street. Bill told me that as a young boy he did a paper round early in the morning and there would be only dry bread in the house; this is all he had before he went off to school. At the age of twelve he worked in a mill in the morning, attending school in the afternoon. His older brother Thomas fought in the First World War and was badly wounded. He was brought back to Scotland, where one of his legs had to be amputated and eventually he was brought home to Collyhurst. Bill told me Thomas was very bitter over what had happened to him (and no wonder!) and to make life even worse, Thomas's girl came one night with his best friend and told him they were getting married. As the months passed he slowly deteriorated and things became so bad that Thomas would allow only Bill to look after him. He would not let even his mother come into the same room. Bill did look after him until he died, still only in his twenties. Annie married, leaving Bill and Lawrence at home with their mother, then Bill married his first wife Agnes at St Patrick's Church, Collyhurst, in 1926. Young Bill was born in the October of 1929 and poor Agnes passed away in 1930. Bill then moved back to his mother's house and Mr and Mrs Webb, Agnes's parents, looked after young Bill whilst his dad was at work.

As time went on I got to know the Webbs, who also lived in Collyhurst, on Reather Street. There were four other daughters and one son and they were a lovely family, really warm and friendly. Taking into consideration it was their daughter who had died, we all got along very well, with never a cross word between us. I remember old Mr Webb saying to me he did not think Bill could ever find anyone better than me to bring up his grandson. I was very touched, it was such a lovely compliment.

Before Bill came to Barlows he had had two jobs. First he was employed at a hat works in Cheetham Hill, delivering goods by horse and cart to various firms. He managed the horse and cart quite easily, but the firm had a car and this was Bill's next target. Unfortunately, he crashed it

and was fired! Then he went to work at ICI in Blackley, leaving them to come to Barlows, where he started on the hoist; in later years he became a packer in the cellar.

When we had any money, Bill and I would go to the Piccadilly picture house. Bill used to love watching Cicely Courtneidge and Jack Hulbert; one song in particular from the film "Jack's the Boy" was called "The flies crawled up the windows". I can still see Bill's expression now – he laughed so much that the tears ran down his face. Personally, I couldn't stand them! My favourites were Laurel and Hardy. By this time we were getting films from America with Rudolph Valentino, the heart throb of many a girl. A good looking man, he starred with Vilma Banky in "The Son of the Sheik" but sadly he died whilst very young after an operation. Some nights, if Bill and I were really flush, after the pictures we would go into Yates's Wine Lodge for a glass of wine and a pork pie. Mostly, though, once Bill had seen me home to Howard Street, he would have to walk back to Collyhurst, as he would not have the tram fare; the miles he must have walked!

On 24th June 1934 my brother Joe got married to Edith at St Michael's Church. They held their reception at the White Lion Hotel. I must have mentioned to Bill that our Joe was getting married, but imagine my surprise when Bill turned up at the White Lion! He did not come into the pub, he was hovering about outside,

Bill Jordan and his first wife, Agnes

when a sharp-eyed cousin of mine who had been in and out of the pub spotted him. She asked him if he was looking for somebody and when she found out who, she nearly fell over herself bringing him in. I had some explaining to do, I can tell you!

After their wedding, Joe and Edith went to live with our cousin Thomas and his wife Annie for a short while. Their house was on the corner of Warde Street and Beaulah Street, Hulme. I think Joe and Edith had a bit of gypsy in their blood, though; after leaving Cousin Thomas's house, they made their first home in Hamilton Street, but didn't stay there long. Their next house was on York Street, then they moved to Lavender Street, then to a house near Chorlton Road and finally to Rex Street in the City Road area. Bill used to help Joe decorate in each of these houses, working through the night to get it all finished. (Flour and water for paste, with more on the floor than was holding the paper up!)

Time was getting on and young Bill was now nearly four. Mrs Jordan was taken poorly early in 1935 and she was ordered into Crumpsall Hospital (now North Manchester General). There were a lot of very confused people in the ward, and sadly Bill's mother died within a few weeks of being admitted. Bill always said afterwards that she had been 'scared' to death; she was only 63 years old. In the next bed to Bill's mother was a very old lady, very very muddled; she

Midday fog in Manchester

didn't speak, only used to spit and snarl at people who went near her. A huge net covered the bed to prevent her getting out. A nurse chatting to us one night said that this old lady belonged to a very wealthy family, and it was some past personal tragedy which had made her the way she was.

Early Married Life

On 8th June 1935 Bill and I were married at St Michael's Church on Lavender Street at 2.30pm. It was a beautiful sunny day and my sister Edna and Bill's brother Lawrence stood for us. Secretly Bill and I both thought Lawrence was after Edna. I wore a pale blue silk dress with short sleeves which I had had made on Stretford Road, a small hat with a veil and blue shoes, and I carried a spray of mixed irises. Bill too looked very smart in a navy blue suit and a white shirt. We had our reception at the White Lion Hotel. Nearly all my family attended and made it a very happy day for us. Mam had spoken to Hartleys and had got us a house in Oswald Street, off York Street, Hulme; we were very happy.

Before we were married Bill had decorated No.8 Oswald Street from top to bottom and I was so proud of our home. Bill put up a fence and gate at the front and we had a tiny garden, plus a large, two-roomed cellar (one room was used to store coal), a back yard and an outside toilet. It was quite a little palace, with gas mantles in each room. The rent was 13s6d (67½p) a week. Bill and young Bill had moved in before we were married. Mr Jones, the rent collector, came one day after Bill had finished decorating, looked at everything and said the house could now be rented out for £1.5.0d (that is, if we were to move out!). Fortunately, the rent was not put up straight away. Bill was still on the hoist earning £2.10.0d (£2.50) and I was in the making up room earning £1.7.6d (£1.37½) per week. Compared to this, my family's life had been hard, and compared to Bill's, we were rich!

After Bill and I were married, we offered Lawrence a home with us but he politely refused, though he used to visit Oswald Street regularly, as did old Mr Webb, whose wife had now died. It was around this time that Mam came round to tell me Uncle Albert had passed away. He was six years older than Mam, and was only 56 when he died. Uncle Albert and Aunt Mary Ann had never left Hulme; after they married they set up home in Owen Street, over towards City Road, where they had ten children. One son when he grew up played a large part in politics. I heard of a death followed by a birth. Edith, my sister-in-law, presented Joe with a beautiful dark-haired baby boy; they had him christened Joseph.

No.8 Oswald Street was a bigger house than Mam's, with three rooms downstairs and three upstairs.

The fireplace in the parlour was black-leaded with a black and silver kerb round it; oilcloth plus a full carpet covered the floor. There was a dark brown three-piece suite, a sideboard, a polished table and gramophone. In the window I had a small table holding a whistling boy.

Bill Jordan junior

The kitchen fireplace was also black-leaded and had two buffets (one at either side), a large oven and a brass rail underneath the mantelpiece. Built in the alcove was a large cupboard with three drawers underneath. In the other alcove there was a desk with two drawers and a book compartment; it had a side shelf which could be pulled out to write letters on. A dresser stood against the opposite wall, then a couch raised at one end, an easy chair, a kitchen table and two upright chairs. The carpet left a surround of oilcloth showing evenly round the room which I used to polish.

In the scullery the fireplace had been boarded up, leaving only the mantelpiece showing, and a new solid iron gas cooker had been put in. There was a sink in the alcove, and a cupboard with green painted doors fitted into the alcove under the window. We had a small table near the cooker, oilcloth covering the floor and a small carpet. There were two doors, one leading to the back yard and one to the cellar, which had a tap so that it could be washed out.

The first bedroom had two alcoves, one containing a cupboard and the other a wardrobe. Bill had brought from his house a dressing table with a large round mirror fitted on to it and a chest of drawers. There was a small fireplace with a fender round it, the bed and oilcloth on the floor. The second bedroom too

Bill and Mary Jordan with Bill's only sister, Annie

had a small fireplace, a dressing table with a large square mirror, one bed and a large bedding chest. Again, oilcloth covered the floor. The third bedroom (box room) had nothing in it until much later and the lobby and stairs were covered in oilcloth; later we had carpet all along. Each room apart from the box room had its own gas mantle fitted on to the wall.

When we moved into Oswald Street the corner with Cooke Street was occupied by a stable where horses were shod. My neighbours were lovely: at No.2 lived Mrs Beech, at No.4 Mrs Jones, No.6 Mrs Loseby, No.10 Maggie Povall (her sister Mrs Annie Curran also lived at No.4 for a time). Mrs Hayour lived at No.12, the Massey family at No.14 and Nos.16 and 18 continually changed. Where Oswald Street met York Street there was a huge pot shop selling pans, pots, ornaments, anything you needed; it was bombed during the Second World War. On the opposite corner to the stable stood St Michael's Church Mission, then an entry leading up to Dryburgh Place, then the Conservative Club (later Sorensen Malt Loaf Company). Next came Drake Street, a corner house which came into Oswald Street occupied by the Gregson family, another entry leading to Dryburgh Place, then a bookshop which was half in Oswald Street and half in York Street (this was also bombed).

Drake Street had houses on both sides leading up to Stretford Road and just after Dryburgh Place there was a pub called the Wheatsheaf.

Cooke Street ran from Rutland Street to Stretford Road.

Starting on the corner of Rutland Street and Cooke Street, there was Hammerton's grocer's, an entry, then the building where Rolls Royce first started and which they still occupied. Houses led up to Dryburgh Place, then one more house and the high class 'Bon Marche' dress shop on the corner of Cooke Street and Stretford Road. The opposite side had a large corner house, the entry behind our houses, the stable on the corner of our street, St Michael's Church Mission, then more houses up to Dryburgh. Two houses stood between this and the corner of Cooke Street and Stretford Road where Currey's shop was. The first three houses next to Rolls Royce were demolished during the Second World War bombing raids on Hulme and the rest had to be pulled down because the bombing had made them structurally unsafe.

It was roundabout 1935 that Mam had some more bad news, this time from her elder sister by 19 years, Aunt Jane Hannah. Despite Mam's being one of the younger children of the family, she was the one everybody turned to with their troubles when things were not going right. Aunt Jane Hannah was a very strict lady, almost hard, and was a rare visitor. When she and Uncle Thomas first married they had lived near to St Philip's Church, but later moved away over to Clayburn Street, Hulme, and never came to Howard Street as the rest of the family did. They had six children to their marriage, the fourth one a daughter they had christened Sarah Ann (but it was pronounced 'Sirann'). She had married a man serving in the Royal Navy and was expecting her first baby. The

Lawrence Jordan

news that Aunt Jane Hannah had sent to Mam was that Sirann had died in childbirth, and the baby with her. She was only in her early twenties and it was so very unexpected and sad. Aunt Jane Hannah had Sirann buried in her wedding dress, with the baby placed in the crook of her arm. Nothing and nobody could console Aunt Jane Hannah. Yet after this very sad event nothing more was heard from her or the family until she herself was dying, then Mam was informed.

As my love was the pictures, Edna's was dancing; she began going when she was about sixteen. She used to go with our cousin Ada (Aunt Ada's daughter) and a few of the girls to Ann Street off City Road, where it cost 6d (2½p) to get in. They also went to the Chorlton Palais, but if I remember rightly the most popular place was Winifred's, which was above Burton's the tailor's on Stretford Road.

A young man who used to go there was keen on our Edna, but unfortunately it was rumoured that he had TB. Such was the fear of this disease in those days that our cousin Ada told Edna, "If you don't find somebody else I'll tell your Mam about him." Some time after this incident the young man did in fact die from consumption.

On one comical occasion, Edna and her friends had been to the Chorlton Palais one evening and on the way home they all started singing as they walked

Cooke Street, with Hammerton's on the Rutland Street corner

along; the popular tune then was 'The Lambeth Walk'. A passing policeman, hearing them, promptly booked them all for "Disturbing the Peace"! When Edna's court case came up she was fined 5s (25p). Still, it never stopped her - she went on dancing. She could do any dance that was going and she really enjoyed it. Cousin Ada and her future husband Alf could also dance, in fact they were nicknamed William Powell and Kay Francis.

Eventually Edna started going out with a Scots lad called Harry, whose family lived in Moss Side: he had one sister and three brothers. Harry was a self-employed building contractor and in later years built up his own business; a smart man, a little like Clark Gable to look at. They made a handsome couple.

One Saturday tea-time in 1936 the paper boys came round the streets shouting, "Special - the King is dying!" I was in the parlour and in my haste to get a paper I pushed the window up so hard that it jammed; it was like that till Bill came home. Being a Royalist, hearing of the King's death was like losing a member of the family.

The same year electricity came to Hulme, and my house and the one next door rented by Mrs Dolly Ryan were the first two in Hulme to have electric lights. Shortly after us, Hammerton's, the grocer's at the corner of Cooke Street and Rutland Street, also had it. Their shop was run by a brother and four sisters and it was spotless. Everything was always fresh, and if the goods were not behind glass cupboard doors, they would be covered with net. There were no fridges then, of course.

The Wheatsheaf, Drake Street

After the King's funeral, Edward was made King, but rumours started because he was very friendly with Mrs Simpson, an American divorcee. I thought it was such a shame he seemed to be hounded; just because she was divorced, that didn't make her a bad woman. He had only been King for eleven months when, towards the end of 1936, he abdicated so that he could marry his Mrs Simpson. I am sure the people would have backed him if he had stood firm - after all, he was head of the Church, and he should have been able to change things.

In the November of 1936 Joe and Edith's son Joey was taken poorly. He started with a cold but didn't seem to improve, and was eventually admitted to Monsall Hospital with diphtheria. That was the Wednesday. Sadly, Joey only lived until the Saturday. He was such a beautiful little boy, only 17 months old,

and it was the end of the world for our Joe and Edith. They had him buried at Southern Cemetery and after the funeral Edith would not go back into their house, so they moved to another house off Princess Road.

At the beginning of 1937 it came to Bill's ears that Lawrence was doing a bit of courting and we were quite thrilled - that is, until we learned the girl's brother was involved with the Communist Party. Bill, always a Labour man, had no time for the Communists and feeling responsible for Lawrence because he was the youngest, he tried to reason with him that this girl was the wrong sort. Alas, Lawrence took no notice, he was so interested in the things her brother had told him. Such was his involvement that in the March of 1937 he joined the 'Red Brigade' and went to fight in the Spanish Civil War. In due course we received five letters from Lawrence. His first, dated 3rd April, came from somewhere in Catalonia - he could not give his full address. It had taken him ten days to get to Spain and he wrote that he was having the best of food and wine, plus ten francs a day (the equivalent of our half crown, now 12½p). Lawrence said the place he was in was really beautiful and he was with people from all walks of life who had given up their careers to fight for peace in Spain - people like teachers, doctors, lawyers, miners and dockers. The second letter, dated 28th April, had on it an address so we could reply. Lawrence was in Albacete; he had moved nearly 400 miles since he had first written and the weather was very hot, in fact he wished for some

Stretford Road in 1958. Bon Marche on the left

"Manchester rain". He wrote about the gunning down of innocent men, women and children, especially the children and asked us to tell little Bill, if he asked where Uncle Lawrence was, that he had gone "in search of the sun". The third letter, dated 8th May from the same address, was a much longer one. He told us of more killings he had witnessed but he still wasn't involved in any fighting. He asked us to send him ten Woodbines as Spanish tobacco was terrible and promised to take us to the Foresters on his first Saturday home. This really upset me, so I know it upset Bill; no matter how he tried he could not understand why Lawrence had done what he had. The fourth letter was a short one, dated 30th May at the same address. Again he complained about the hot weather and the flies but said he was in good health. He and another man were in a dugout about four feet deep; there was no wallpaper on the walls and the neighbours were quite noisy - that was his sense of humour. He told us he had had a few letters from home from various people and asked if we were following the Spanish situation in the newspapers. He closed by saying things were hotting up and soon everything would be sorted out and he would be home.

It was August before we heard any more, and then it was a letter from the Communist Party of Great Britain, dated 20th August 1937:

"Dear Friend,
            It is our sad responsibility to have to convey

Postcard sent by Lawrence Jordan from Spain

to you news received from the Headquarters of the British Battalion fighting in the Spanish Government Army, that Comrade L Jordan has been killed in recent fighting near Madrid.

Comrade Jordan and others fell in the course of the victorious advance against Franco's Fascist forces, an advance which is the guarantee of ultimate victory over Franco.

We wish to convey to you our sincere and deep sympathy with you in the great loss you have suffered in the death of our comrade Jordan; his memory as a gallant fighter for peace and democracy will always be honoured."

The death note which followed

Brother Joe's son, Joey, photographed the year before he died in 1936

Burton's on Stretford Road in 1959. Winifred's Dance Studio was above the shop

stated that Lawrence died of wounds on 14th July at Brunete, Spain. I thought Bill was going to go out of his mind, such was his grief. Can you imagine how we felt when two weeks later we received a letter from Lawrence? The address and date were missing. Lawrence wrote saying he could not see why Bill was against what he was doing, and he told Bill not to lose any sleep about it. He went on to say he was not in Spain for the fun of it, it was something he believed in and he would much prefer to be living a normal life. The previous day a trench mortar had hit his dugout and one lad from Hulme had been killed, but he didn't really write much about what was happening generally except to say that the fall at Bilboa was a bad blow.

He did describe one incident, though. A boxing match had been arranged in the village between the British Battalion and the villagers, and everyone had apparently turned out for this. It had been in progress for about half an hour when seven government planes came over and there was a stampede of people all trying to escape. Lawrence said he held one little girl and tried in the bit of Spanish he had learned to comfort her; he wrote, "I shall never forget the look of terror on that tiny Spanish face." Many were killed that day.

Bill was beside himself when he received the letter; he contacted every person he could think of who might have any power because it made him believe Lawrence was alive. Alas, nothing came of his enquiries and in the end he had to give up and accept the inevitable, but it was very hard for him. Lawrence was a lovely young man.

Bill was very interested in politics and before we were married he used to attend all the Labour meetings near his home on Rochdale Road. The Labour MP for Bill's district then was a Mr Johnnie Clynes, who had held his seat for twenty years. He lost it in 1931 after much publicity surrounding his wish to be one of the MPs "standing by" at a Royal birth. (Princess Margaret was born the year before.) Rumour had it he preferred to be away with the gentry than looking after his own constituents. After we had married, Bill's interest continued. He attended all the meetings at the Zion Chapel on Stretford Road and he aired his views. For someone who had not had a very good education, he knew what he was talking about, and people would always listen to what he had to say.

Bill even went to hear Oswald Mosley, founder of the British Union of Fascists, speak at the Free Trade Hall, but just as his feelings towards the Communist Party bordered on hatred after what had happened to Lawrence, so he had no time for the Fascists or what they stood for either. After one of Mosley's meetings there was a big fight outside the Free Trade Hall on Peter Street. Cars were overturned and lots of people were arrested, in fact some innocent people were taken away. By then Bill had lost interest in Mosley, but he continued going to the Zion Institute for many years and remained a keen Labour man all his life.

In June 1937 we had our first holiday, thanks to someone Bill knew who recommended a boarding house on the Isle of Man at Douglas. Young Bill was

Mary Jordan and Cousin Mary in Howard Street

now nearly eight, and so he would not be lonely we took Aunt Ada's youngest daughter Mary with us; Bill and Mary got along very well with each other. We caught the 8.00am train from Manchester Victoria Station to Liverpool, then the boat to Douglas. Once on board I was terrified and Bill bought me a book to take my mind off the crossing. I think he must have picked up the first one he saw without reading the title – it was called "Down to the Sea in Ships"! Still, he meant well.

Arriving at 3.30pm, we went straight to Mrs Cottier's boarding house overlooking Douglas Bay. On the day you arrived, you were allowed to enter the house by the front door. After that, you could only use the back door, which was on a level with the TT race course. It was a lovely place, though Mrs Cottier was a very strict lady and you would only be allowed in the boarding house at meal times. Nearly all the other guests were retired people and Bill and Mary were the only children. All day long they would be normal children, but the minute we went in for our meals they seemed to go daft and many a kick passed under the table to try and control them, whilst Bill and I would smile sweetly at the other guests.

Johnnie Clynes (centre) canvassing in Miles Platting in 1931

On the first day there Bill managed to fall into the fountain at Douglas Head, but it was a lovely week and we could not have wished for a nicer boarding house or for better weather. However, on our journey home the crossing was very rough and the sailors put sheets over the sides of the boat to try and steady her; unfortunately one sailor was lost overboard.

Towards the end of 1937 Edna and Harry decided to marry and their wedding took place at St Michael's Church on Boxing Day; our Joe gave Edna away, as Dad had passed on. They made a lovely-looking couple; Harry had a light bluish suit (a very up-to-the-minute colour) and Edna had a full length blue satin wedding gown with long sleeves tapering to a point at the wrist. She wore a sequined 'Juliet cap' from Jackson's on Stretford Road and silver shoes. As it was a Christmas wedding, flowers were hard to get, but her bouquet of hyacinths was lovely and the reception at the White Lion Hotel was a really good do. They didn't have their own home straight away, but lived with Harry's parents in Moss Side.

Mam was now finally on her own. Each evening after tea I used to slip round to see her and sometimes, looking back, I think we spent more time in her house than we did in ours. On the way home I used to call in at the chip shop on York Street and get a pennorth of chips and a 2d fish. Mam looked after young Bill whilst Bill and I were at work and he went everywhere with her; on wet days he was tucked under her shawl.

Young Bill attended St Wilfrid's RC School on Rutland Street and was absolutely football mad. What a lad! Every week it was either new trousers or new shoes. Yet he was a very quiet lad and very attached to his dad, perhaps because of his early years. And he was another one for picking up every illness going; Mam used to say, "The wind has only to blow on him." Still, he grew up to be a fine man. He played football for Howard Rangers, a local team, and many years later he even had a trial for Manchester United.

Bill used to make me laugh with his tales. Apparently when he first came to Manchester his Blackburn accent was very strong and the boys in Colly-hurst used to take the Mickey out of him. In any daft games, Bill would be the "stoogie". One of their tricks was for two boys to pretend to be fighting when they all came out of school. The other boys would gather round and when some passing adult came to split them up, one of the boys was supposed to fall on the floor. The day dawned when it was Bill's turn and down he fell, only to go face first into a puddle of dirty water. Trust Bill!

Another game was to put a cat in a sack, then go round the houses knocking on the doors. If a man answered, they would ask, "Do you want any fire-wood?" as normally a man's answer would be "No". But if a woman answered, she would nearly always buy something because the children looked so scruffy and she would take pity. The idea was that when the woman said, "Yes," they would open the bag and of course out sprang the cat, scaring the wits out of the woman. Bill got it wrong again! A man answered his knock and Bill opened the

Bill and Mary Jordan, 10/7/37

sack. You can imagine what happened next - the man chased Bill up and down the streets, shouting, "I'll bet thee a bob I catch thee," and so he did, giving Bill a good hiding. After that I don't think Bill was so eager to join in their games. Children can be so cruel.

If Bill was ratty, just to annoy me he would say, "Your mam might have taught to how to look after the house, to clean and wash and rear the children, but she could not teach you to cook like her." His words were very true. Mam was an excellent cook and I certainly never took after her. Another of Bill's sayings if things weren't going right was "Burst the cat", or "Blimey"; perhaps his parents said these things.

We had been in Oswald Street nearly two years when somebody told Bill there was an empty house in Tipper Street near York Street. He went to see it, accepted it and by the time I went to see it he had started to decorate. It was then I discovered that the previous occupants had been the Healeys ("Skenning Ben" was one of their sons). The house was very nice and it seemed a nice street, but because of who had lived there before I told Bill I wouldn't have it. Poor Bill, he couldn't understand. Tears followed but finally we stayed in Oswald Street. It's funny how a person from the past can change your opinion. No way

Sister Edna

Harry Dunn, Edna's husband

would I have moved into that house.

In 1938 Joe and Edith were living near Princess Road and Edith was expecting their second baby. The place was terrible, overrun with mice and beetles. On 25th March they were blessed with another son and this one they called Brian with Joseph as his second name. What a scallywag he turned out to be as he grew up! But he was such a lovable little boy, full of mischief. Another one for Mam to take under her shawl. They moved shortly after Brian's birth to Bridge Street, off Higher Cambridge Street and near the dental hospital, but again they only stayed there for a short time. Next they took over a confectionery shop round the corner from Bridge Street. Edith used to run the shop while Joe was at work. Things went well for a while with them, but World War Two was looming (though nobody wanted to believe we would have another war at that time). Sadly, because people did not have the money, the shop started running at a loss and they had to close it.

Their last move was to a house off Cambridge Street. Edith was a lovely woman with a heart of gold. If anyone were to admire something she had, she would give it to them, and not just within the family – anybody. Her family were always borrowing one thing or another and this caused arguments between them. Perhaps that's one of the reasons they moved as often as they did.

Bill bought our first wireless from Smarts on Victoria Street, Deansgate and it brought us lots of enjoyment. The only trouble was, it ran off batteries and you could guarantee that just when an exciting part came up, the battery would fade away. It was infuriating! We had to take the battery for recharging to the dog meat shop on the corner of Gay Street. Some nights Mam would come round to listen to the stories and we had to have it rather loud so Mam could hear, but my neighbours understood and this didn't happen every night. Bill would always walk Mam home and make sure everything was OK.

Each evening there would be a different dance band playing – Oscar Rabin, Geraldo and Joe Loss were popular at that time – and in later years we used to enjoy "Hancock's Half Hour", Jewel and Wariss and Bebe Daniels and Ben Lyon. For a really chilling story I used to listen to "The Man in Black" on the Home Service. With the lights switched off and only the blaze from the fire, that really chilled you to the bone. How the youngsters today would laugh!

Sometimes on a Saturday night Mam, Bill and I would go for a drink for the 'last hour' in the Railway Guard on the corner of Bedford Street and Hazel Street. (In those days, of course, the pubs closed at 10.00pm.) In later years we went to the Foresters Arms on the corner of Welcomb Street and George Street, a lovely friendly little pub run by Mr Jack Higgins – in fact it was nicknamed "Higginses".

By now Edna and Harry had their first baby, a little girl born on 22nd April and called June. She was the apple of Harry's eye; nothing was too good for her.

Our second holiday, again to the Isle of Man, was in 1938 (Scots week). This time we stayed at a boarding house at 122 Bucks Road, a lovely place. Our Joe and Edith had already been there a week when we arrived and they were staying over until the Monday. After we had settled in on the Saturday, Joe said he would show us the sights – he'd forgotten we had been there before. The Sunday was a beautiful day and we all went down to Onchan Head, where there is a huge tower similar to Blackpool Tower and at the top a cafe called the Outside Inn.

Across the road from where we were staying was the Rose Mount public house and before Joe and Edith had to leave on the Monday we went in for a drink. This was the place where I had my first glass of champagne, for Joe had bought a bottle to celebrate their having been blessed with another baby. Truthfully, I didn't think much of the champagne.

Bill and I, with young Bill and Cousin Mary, went one further time to the Isle of Man the year after. Again we stayed on Bucks Road but at a different number and it was a dreadful place! We had a room at the top of the house, very pokey and with the dimmest of light bulbs. Considering how much they charged, it was shocking, a real disappointment compared to our two previous visits.

The Darkest Years

1939 brought a lot of changes for everybody. Hulme was starting to alter as houses were now being classed as slums and were being knocked down. They were starting to build three storey flats on Jackson Street, between George Street and Clarendon Street, but the War brought that to a halt. Aunt Eliza's house on Kingston Street was demolished and sadly we lost touch. Somebody told Mam Aunt Eliza had gone back to Swinton, but despite many enquiries we never saw her or the children again. It was a shame because we had always got along so well.

1939 also brought talk of a second World War. People did not want to believe it, but Hitler appeared to be a very powerful man then, judging by what he had already accomplished abroad. But we were happy. Young Bill was going on

Bill Jordan and Mary's brother Joe in the Isle of Man

ten and growing rapidly. In the June of that year I was expecting our first baby. As my time approached I had had a trouble free pregnancy. Everything that could be bought had been bought; everything was ready.

Then one day I had terrible backache nearly all day and Bill was so concerned he went for the midwife. I can see her now, very brisk, telling me to stop feeling sorry for myself. She made a brief examination and then ordered Bill to go and fetch a doctor. Young Doctor Burke was now working with his father and he came to see me, bringing Bill back with him in his car. He too examined me, then said, "I will go and fetch my father." When Old Doctor Burke arrived, after only minutes he said briskly, "Ambulance. This woman is an emergency case." I said I would not go into hospital and he just turned to Bill and said, "Take no notice of this woman, she's mad." I was rushed to St Mary's Hospital on Whitworth Street, which was for emergency admissions only in those days.

For two days nothing happened. To help with the pain I was given gas and air, but not by today's methods - I had to press a pump up and down to release the gas and air myself. On 3rd June 1939 all hope was abandoned for the men trapped in the submarine Thetis, stuck in the mud beneath Liverpool Bay, and all next day in hospital the wireless played "Eternal Father, strong to save". My spirits were very low for all the sailors who had lost their lives and for their families. Little did I know what was in store for me.

Doctors came and went, then they decided I would have to have an operation. Our baby daughter was born, and was stillborn. Up to just before the operation there had been a heartbeat, but she didn't survive the trauma of birth. Only somebody who has been in this kind of situation will understand how I felt.

They say you have to be cruel to be kind. A few days after I had lost my baby, a nurse brought me a baby and a bottle, saying this baby had lost its mother, so I could comfort it and it would comfort me. Bill was shattered. So often people only seem to direct their sympathies towards the mother, but the fathers obviously feel as bad.

The girls from Barlows came and visited and trying to cheer me up, informed me that

Barlows were having a picnic soon. Most of the hospital staff were very nice to me and there were three doctors looking after me: Doctor Fletcher Shaw, a fine big man, the lady doctor Iris Spencer and Doctor Lawler. Doctor Lawler came every morning to see me and you could see the nurses almost pushing each other over so that they could stand by his side. He was extremely good looking, a little younger than Doctor Fletcher Shaw. Two Irish nurses, both very pretty, attended me and did everything together. One patient in the ward had apparently christened them "Nervo and Knox" and the nickname had stuck. From my bed I could see down Oxford Road and near the Refuge building there was a bus stop. Each evening I would see one of the girls from Barlows waiting there to go home. Bill came every day to visit me, as did my family and friends. After three weeks I was allowed to go home. On the whole people were kind, but everything I bought I gave away; I could not bear any reminders of what might have been.

On 22nd July 1939 Harry came to Mam's house to tell us Edna had given birth to a little boy and they were calling him Harry. I cannot explain how I felt. Of course I was pleased for Edna and Harry but so very upset that our baby had not lived. To look at Harry you would have thought no man had ever had a son before, he was so proud of the little fellow. That week Young Doctor Burke recommended I go on the picnic from work, as it might take my mind off the things that had happened. We went to Southport

on that occasion and everybody was so kind to me. At the end of July I returned to work at Barlows.

War

Germany had invaded Poland, so on 3rd September 1939 Great Britain and France declared war against Germany. Number 8 Oswald Street was semi-closed and we all moved back to Mam's. Our nearest air raid shelter was on Great Jackson Street near the police station.

The shelters, although life-saving necessities, were very cold places, damp and dreary and very unhygienic in some ways. In the beginning we had to take our own candles and chairs. It's funny to think of now, but was terrifying at the time. The atmosphere was terrible and you could feel the fear in people as the night progressed. People would come in from the pubs at closing time, some a little worse for drink, then the arguments would start. Sometimes I used to wonder if it was worse down in the shelters or at home in your own house, even taking into consideration that your house could be hit.

It was just after New Year 1940 that we heard our Edna's little boy Harry was not well. He had contracted meningitis and on 6th January he died at home in our Edna's arms. What a terrible thing to happen to any woman! Edna and Harry were heartbroken and no words could be found to give them any comfort. In fact, Harry seemed to change after this and never really came to terms with his loss. Little Harry was laid to

Welcomb Street in 1933, the Foresters Arms on the left

rest at Southern Cemetery. Later that year, in September, our Edna had her third baby, a little girl they had christened Edna.

Just after the war had started and of course between the air raids we were having, people could go down to the gasworks on Medlock Street where a German plane was on display for several weeks. It didn't actually come down there, it was only for people to look at and if I remember rightly, there was a charge of 3d to see it. On close inspection you could see the gaping holes where the bullets had gone through. You were only supposed to walk round it, but some people tried to climb in for a closer inspection.

At work Albert Lea, whom I have already mentioned, was bringing a cage truck full of material up from the cellar to the making up room. When he got in the hoist with the truck the cage caught on the side of the hoist as Albert pressed the button for the cage to go up, and he was trapped against the walls. The fire brigade was called and eventually Albert was released and taken to Manchester Royal Infirmary, where they found he had a broken leg and some internal injuries. He was in the hospital for a long time, at first very poorly. We all visited him regularly, keeping him informed of what was happening at Barlows and any other snippets of information that might cheer him up. It took a long time but eventually he did recover and return to Barlows.

Weeks went into months and the stories one heard were terrible. How could Hitler do the things he was doing? It was then decided all children had to be evacuated from towns at risk. Young Bill had to go and he was sent to a couple who lived

at Great Harwood. I will not mention the name because the man was quite a big business-man in the Manchester area and possibly now one of his sons is carrying on the family firm. It was heart-breaking sending young Bill away, he was such a little scrap, but we thought we were doing the right thing at that time. The woman's mother, a retired schoolteacher, lived with them and from what we could gather it was she that young Bill was left with during the day when the couple were at work.

We went each weekend to see him and we knew he was desperately unhappy; the hope on his little face that we would be taking him home would be followed by disappointment when he knew we weren't. It was bitterly cold weather but we were never allowed to stay in the house, we had to take young Bill for a walk round the town. We were sometimes given a cup of tea before we left, but that was rare.

One week Bill received a letter from the man saying young Bill had misbehaved himself and had had to be chastised, and off we went to see what had happened. On our arrival, we were told that young Bill had had something in his hand and the older woman wanted to know what it was. Young Bill had refused to tell her and con-sequently the son-in-law had slapped Bill's face, saying he was being cheeky. Well, that was more than enough for my husband! This was our ideal opportunity and he said, "We are taking young Bill home regardless of the war." We both wondered afterwards if young Bill had been smacked on more than that occasion and being such a quiet lad, had been scared to tell us. Anyway, he was home again, going around with his loving grandma, tucked beneath her shawl.

Sister Edna with her daughters June and Edna

Living with War

As the war progressed there were many changes for everyone. Bill left Barlows and went to work at Metrovicks in Trafford Park; he also became a volunt-ary ARP warden. Bombay House, one of the buildings on Whitworth Street which Barlows owned, had to be closed as there wasn't the work for the staff. Some of the people came to work at Barlows in Chepstow Street, while others like Rosie May and Beattie Ackerley left Chepstow Street to join the ATS. Rosie May called in to work once when she was home on leave and then unfortunately we lost touch.

Because of the shortage of things during the war years, anybody with iron had to give it up and we lost our gate and fencing from Oswald Street. In fact anything made from iron had to be surrendered: iron boilers, iron bedsteads and so on. Nobody was given any compensation for the things taken, but we all agreed if it helped the war effort it was well worth it. Edna's husband Harry was called up and sent with the Forces to Italy, though he did get a couple of leaves. They had left his mother's house by then for their own house in Grafton Street near to Brooks's Bar. Our Joe was called up and from the Army he joined the Pioneer Corps. After a brief training at Huyton, Liverpool, he was sent all over England, clearing up after the bombings and later he

The first "Manchester" bomber at Metrovicks, completed at the end of December 1940 and destroyed during the Blitz

was sent to Germany. It must have seemed like a recurring nightmare for Mam, seeing her family one by one going to war again.

Among the things I will never forget about the war years were the radio broadcasts by William Joyce, "Lord Haw Haw", an Englishman who had gone over to Germany. He used to open with the words, "Germany calling, Germany calling." Whenever he had been on the radio, you could guarantee a raid would start after he had finished speaking. He had been on just before the terrible blitz on Manchester. Once he started talking about parks, saying how much he loved our parks and how well he knew them. He knew where Buile Hill Park was and Heaton Park and Hullard Park, but the nicest park of all for him was Trafford Park. The next day we learned why he had said all this. Bill was on continuous 24-hour shifts at Metrovicks to try and complete their work, which was on bomber planes. That night in December 1940 Trafford Park was hit. It had been the hive of Manchester's industry and everything was ruined in just a few hours. Along with many other companies, Metrovicks was hit badly and all the bomber planes destroyed. The incendiaries were smouldering for weeks afterwards.

After Bill had finished his day work he would be out at night on patrol. Some nights I never knew where he was, or even if he was safe. When Portland Street was hit, Bill was there. This was near Christmas time when Piccadilly, Deansgate, Market Street and Portland Street had taken a real hammering, and buildings were either destroyed or badly damaged in all the surrounding areas. Some of the warehouses were still burning the next day.

Joe Hopwood, a voluntary ARP man at Barlows who had come from Tootal Broadhurst, was in the fire service and he was helping to fight one of the fires at the top end of Portland Street near to Piccadilly when he fell into the flames. He left a wife and two small children. So many people lost their lives in Manchester by just trying to help others.

Hulme was no longer anything like Hulme. The Town Hall, a fine old building on Stretford Road, had been hit and was nearly ruined. On the corner of Stretford Road and Clopton Street there was a Timpson's shoe shop, still standing after the raid but with the windows

blown out. There was debris everywhere and people, believe it or not, were searching through all of this to try and find shoes that matched! Poverty was so rife in those days, it's unbelievable what people would do to get hold of things. All Saints Church and the Church of the Holy Name, both on Oxford Road, were bombed during this raid and the Manchester Royal Infirmary was also hit. A nurse was killed and part of the top floor demolished. If you look now at the Infirmary, you will find that part of the building has two floors, the rest three; this was the result of the bombings.

Barlows took a warehouse on Princess Street and because of his reputation as an all rounder who knew everything there was to know about the workings of a warehouse, Mr Albert Lea was moved to these new premises. One morning during the blackout he was walking down Princess Street, going to open the place for the day, when a traction engine lost control and mounted the pavement, killing him instantly. These were huge vehicles and Albert didn't stand a chance. His death came as a great shock to everybody - I don't think there was anyone who didn't like Albert - but to me it seemed really to hit home. Albert had always been so kind to me, taken me under his wing, so to speak, when I first started work, just like a second Dad. His death was a big blow to the warehouse trade.

Our Joe was still being sent from place to place; the sights he had to endure! After one of the terrible raids on Manchester Joe met Mr Wendell Wilkie, the Vice President of America, and

shook hands with him in Piccadilly, near the statue of Queen Victoria.

One morning, emerging from the shelters after a particularly heavy raid, we found that a string of bombs which had started at Moss Lane and finished at Ardwick Green had nearly demolished Hulme. We went round to Number 8 Oswald Street to find that the front of our house had been hit and was half down; there were no windows or chimneys. Worse was to come in Cooke Street. A gas main had gone and Mrs Bateman's house had blown up, killing her and three children. Victoria Street had been a direct hit and half the street was flattened. Families had been wiped out, yet in the door frame of one house - all that was left of it - the fan light over the front door still had the glass intact with a crucifix still attached.

It was a terrible time and the smell of the fires which had been put out lingered for weeks. The air was murky and people were stunned, trying desperately to carry on and pick up the pieces of their lives but all the time fearing when the next siren would go. During these years, as I have said, Bill was working at Metrovicks; he had left Barlows for a better wage and was employed in the engineering shop making parts for guns. After the blitz on Trafford Park, he was transferred to the Salford branch, but this was just like going from one building to another. So close were Manchester and Salford that parts of the Park did spill over into Salford.

As the war dragged on, men were being continually called up and a lot from Barlows had

Wendell Wilkie in Manchester. Joe is in the centre

to go. By the end of 1941 labour was very short and so single women and childless widows aged between 19 and 30 were also called up. They could either go into the Forces or into a factory to do war work, and they could only be excused if they had children below the age of fourteen. Things were looking really bad. Manchester had been hit so badly we did not have enough men to cope with it all. Exchange and Victoria Stations had both been damaged; it was hard to believe this had once been a fine city. Nearly every family with men of a certain age had somebody fighting in the war one way or another. Three of Aunt Ada's sons were abroad. Thomas and Herbert met up whilst in the desert and there was a photograph of them in the Manchester Evening News. Their other brother, Henry, was a sergeant in the Royal Air Force. When he was 22, his plane hit a mountain and he was killed. No home funeral for him; he was buried in Turin, Northern Italy. Another cross for Aunt Ada to bear.

By 1941 rationing was a way of life. Sugar, tea, bacon and fat were the first to be rationed. Later the meat ration was fixed at 1s2d (6p) per head per week, but dried and evaporated milk and tinned meat had started coming over from the States. Each item was worth a certain number of "points" and people would have to queue for everything and then sometimes be disappointed. Again that year Manchester was hit: the Gaiety and the Theatre Royal picture houses were damaged, as was the centre of Piccadilly.

But worst affected was the Salford Royal Hospital; there several nurses were killed. How could they allow hospitals to be bombed? It was during these terrible months I realised I was expecting another baby. Unlike my first pregnancy, this time I did not buy anything, perhaps because things were all rationed or maybe because of the fear that the same thing could happen to me again. Still, my family were very good, especially Mam.

In March 1942 I had my second baby, this time born in Withington Hospital and yet another panic admission. Old Doctor Burke had long since retired, but Young Doctor Burke attended me. In those days Caesarean sections were not performed, so after a long labour and many blood transfusions he was born. At the time neither of us was expected to live and a vicar was brought. He asked me what I wanted the baby called and I said the first names that came into my head, Brian Lawrence. (Around that time there was an Australian singer called Brian Lawrance, but we liked the name Brian anyway and I think I picked Lawrence because of Bill's younger brother.) The baby was christened there and then and three weeks later we were both allowed home.

Although Brian was christened in the hospital, I still had him done at the Church. The vicar of St Michael's was going to christen him and we asked my brother Joe, home on leave, to be Brian's godfather. One of Mam's neighbours and a good friend to our family, Mrs

Son Brian and Nephew Brian

Brindley, was Brian's god-mother. However, we arrived at St Michael's a few minutes late and the vicar (who only had one leg and was permanently bad-tempered) stopped talking as we entered the church; he was already performing a baptism. He pointed his finger down the aisle at us and shouted, "Wait there!" He finished christening the child and then came down the aisle to us, but before we could apologise for being late he said, "You are late! You cannot expect me to perform another baptism now, so come back next Wednesday." This without giving us a chance to explain anything. That was enough for Bill; he turned round and walked out of the church. Joe didn't. He said, "Where I have come from, if we have a job to do we have to do it, otherwise we would be in serious trouble and it could cost lives. We cannot lay down our arms because somebody is late," and with that he walked out. The vicar didn't say anything about Joe's outburst. I later went to see the vicar at St Stephen's Church on City Road and Brian was christened on Wednesday, 12th April 1942.

The Roman Catholic Church is more lenient today than it was in the 1940s. In my early married life the priest from St Wilfrid's Church often came to our house, but only when Bill was at work. He repeatedly told me I was living in sin and that if I would go round to the church any evening with Bill, he would re-marry us and all would be well. Bill had married me at St Michael's (Church of England) but he had not changed his faith. I didn't expect him to, nor he me; it just never came up. Things went from bad to worse after I had had Brian. As well as

Cooke Street

telling me I was living in sin, the priest then started to add, "Your son is illegitimate." It was very upsetting and I didn't want to have to tell Bill about the priest, because young Bill was attending St Wilfrid's School. Eventually, I am glad to say, this man left the parish and the one who took his place was as different again. He often came and had a cup of tea with me and he never once mentioned our different religions.

One Saturday afternoon I was stoning the front steps at Oswald Street when a pack of dogs came racing down the street, all over my cleaning and nearly taking me and the bucket with them as they ran off. When they had gone and I had repaired the damage I noticed a little dog crouched by the wall, shivering. It was an ordinary little dog apart from what looked like a white cross on its forehead. Quite without thinking, I said, "Come on, Bobby." He hesitated for a moment, then in he ran without a second glance and lay down in front of the fire. Bobby turned out to be a good and faithful dog. He would run and hide under the couch and when he did this we would always know that within a few minutes the sirens would go; strange how he knew.

As time went on, more and more shelters were being built,

practically one on every street now. The war showed no signs of coming to an end. All the houses between Medlock Street and Duke Street and from River Street to Clarendon Street had been pulled down and shelters were built there. The rationing was terrible; you would get word from a neighbour that such and such a shop had such an item, off you would go to queue and sometimes it would all be in vain. Whatever it was they had had, would have already gone. You were only allowed something like 2oz of tea, 2oz of butter and 2oz of sugar a week, and perhaps one egg every two weeks. Cigarettes had to be queued for always (Bill smoked like a trooper) and when you did get them, they would be in fives and American brands. Still, to the smoker a cigarette was a cigarette. Clothing cost so many coupons that new clothes fast became a luxury; it was a case of "make do and mend". Sometimes people managed to get clothes and then they would sell them for coupons, but by buying things that way you were paying twice.

Casualties

Baby Brian was coming up to nine months of age when he caught pneumonia. To see a baby so ill, gasping for his breath, skin wet and a strange

colour, was bad enough for anybody but for me, his mother, it was like the end of the world. Young Doctor Burke had been treating him at home but in the end he had to send Brian into Booth Hall Hospital, where, thank God, he fully recovered. Some months later we had another scare when he was admitted again, and again with suspected pneumonia. Fortunately, this time it was a false alarm.

On 28th March 1943 young Bill was 13 and he was confirmed at St Wilfrid's Church; he had always walked with them round the parish at Whit Week, kitted out in his new clothes. He picked the name Joseph as his confirmation name (our Joe had been good to all our children).

Before Brian's second birthday we had all gone round to Mam's for tea. She still did all her cooking on the open fire and there was always a roaring blaze. Bill was standing in the middle of the room with his back to the fire and young Brian was running round and round his dad's legs when suddenly he tripped over, hands stretching out in front of him as he fell, and both hands landed on the oven door, which was red hot; his screams were pitiful. Bill immediately picked him up and was off to the Manchester Royal Infirmary. They finally returned to Mam's house after ten o'clock that night. Brian's hands had been dressed and the doctor had said that as far as he could see, there shouldn't be any permanent damage. I had to take Brian to the Gartside Street Clinic every morning for several weeks to have his hands freshly dressed, but luckily he made a full recovery. My brother Joe was home on leave and when he heard what had happened to our Brian he went on City Road to a shop next door to Doctor Burke's surgery where they sold toys. He bought our Brian a red tin car with pedals, much too big for him at the time, but he soon learned how to make it go and had many hours of pleasure from it.

One morning I was out queuing for food when I heard some women behind me talking about the previous night's raids. Hearing them mention that Cambridge Street and the surroundings had been hit very badly, my ears pricked up. Our Joe's wife Edith lived there and so did my ex-fiance John; he and his wife had a house down near the dental hospital. After asking these women a few questions I learnt all the streets near the dental hospital had been hit. I hurried home

Bomb crater among the air raid shelters in St George's Park

to tell Bill and my mam what I had heard. Joe had returned to the Army and Mam was very worried about Edith and Brian as she had not seen them since Joe had gone back. After hearing what I had to say, she voiced her fears. Our Edna's husband was still home on leave so he and Bill went off to Edith's. They couldn't get any answer to their knock, but could hear Brian's voice crying out. Harry did no more than climb in through a window which had been left open, and there was Brian alone in the house. They brought him back to Mam's where she and I looked after him until Joe's next leave. Edith was nowhere to be found; she had gone away, leaving Brian in the hope somebody would come and find him. Thank God we did!

The next night their row of houses was flattened. The day after, Bill and I went to where John had lived, only to find nothing – no houses, no visible roads, and hardly any of the streets left standing. We heard the survivors had been taken to Manchester Royal. On enquiring, we found Laura, John's wife, had been admitted. Laura told us that on the night of the raid, her nephew and his fiancee were at the house when it had been hit. They were both dead. Laura had been blown to the bottom of the cellar steps, landing on her feet and with not a scratch or mark on her. John, she went on to tell us, had not yet been found. It was two days later when the workmen trying to clear the debris found him buried under a load of rubble; he had been blown right out of the house. He had numerous injuries and was in the hospital for months having operation after operation. It was during this time that Laura deteriorated. All her nerves went through the shock of what had happened and sadly she passed away. Bill, Mam and I used to take it in turns to visit John. His progress was slow, due to all his injuries, but eventually he did come out of hospital and start to pick up the pieces of his life.

Towards the end of the war, Metrovicks stopped some of the extra staff they had taken on and Bill was one of them. He got another job, still in Trafford Park but this time on a building site, steel erecting. While he was there he got to know a chap who rarely spoke to anybody, just got on with his work, but he seemed to take to Bill. It was a hot summer's day and the men on the building site had taken off their shirts whilst they were

working, including Bill, but this chap didn't. When Bill asked him about this, the man did take off his shirt and showed Bill his back. There were ugly scars right across it from the neck to the waistline. The man then quickly put his shirt back on before anyone else saw him. He told Bill his family had some time before fallen on hard times and one day, because they were so desperately hungry and he had no money, he had stolen a loaf of bread. He had been caught and given the birch instead of a prison sentence and that was why he would never take off his shirt. This affected Bill deeply. He too had known hard times and although what the man had done was wrong, he was basically a good man and Bill said he hadn't deserved the birch. Bill did not stay on the site for long. He was offered a job back at Barlows and he worked this time in the cellar, packing, loading and unloading the goods. The cellar manager at that time was a Mr Wheatley and he told me he had

never met a man who could work as hard and as quickly as Bill did.

One evening Bill and I took our Brian and my nephew Brian to the Hulme Hippodrome. How they enjoyed it! On coming out, my nephew Brian, running as usual, was in front of us. When you came out of the Hippodrome, you came down a long ramp to the street, made up from wooden boards which ran crosswise. Running down the slope, Brian gathered speed. Suddenly he decided to look back, probably to see where we were and in doing so he caught the toe of his shoe between the boards. Down he went, face first! By the time we had reached him somebody had already picked him up. He was screaming, all his face was cut and we couldn't seem to see his left eye because of all the blood; he looked awful! Bill told me to take our Brian home and he took my nephew Brian to Manchester Royal Infirmary. Later Brian was allowed home, a sorry sight, all bruised and

Bill Jordan at Barlow's loading bay

cut. But come the next day he was off again, running everywhere.

Young Bill was due to start work; he had reached the age of 15. In Barlows building there were quite a few other firms and one which Barlows did work for was Olivo and Bakirgian. I was involved in a lot of their work and so got to know the staff quite well, and one day whilst I was down in their offices I asked one of the men if they had any jobs which would be suitable for our Bill. I think because they knew me they took him on, first as a general errand boy and later they trained him in all the ways of the cloth industry. Bill was there for many many years, in fact until the firm closed down.

Picking up the Pieces

When the war had officially ended, it felt as if a huge weight had been lifted from everybody's shoulders. Every street in Hulme had a party for the children. Union Jacks hung from the window sills and all the windows were dressed up with red, white and blue bunting. Each house brought out a table and they were placed end to end down the middle of the street, forming a long chain. Neighbours had clubbed together and any spare food they had in the house was brought out. It was a lovely day for both the children and the adults. Any child who got a bit out of hand was given a good-humoured clout. Although it was a happy day, everyone so relieved the war had ended, there were many who had lost a loved one and there were tears as well as smiles.

In 1945 we managed to get a little money together and we decided to have a week's holiday. At the last minute Bill could not get the time off from work, so off I went with our Brian and my nephew Brian to Blackpool. Our Bill was now in his sixteenth year and felt he was too old to come with us. I had got the address of a boarding house that welcomed children (some didn't) out of the Manchester Evening News and it turned out to be lovely, really like home. The weather that week was glorious and we would go down to the beach every day. The two boys loved it and because we had had such a good time, before we left I booked for the following year.

On our visit the next year we found that the boarding house had changed hands, but the new owners were very pleasant. Bill said we would take the two Brians to the funfair. What a day it turned out to be! We couldn't get either of them out of the fun house and in the end I think we had literally to drag them away. The following day we were all on the beach and nephew Brian took our Brian to watch the Punch and Judy man. That finished at nearly lunch time and my nephew came racing back. (I don't think he ever walked.) But when Bill asked him where our Brian was, he didn't know. The sky had suddenly clouded over, people were going back to their digs for dinner and our Brian was nowhere to be seen. The heavens opened and soon we were the only people on the beach.

I don't know if it's still the same now, but in those days there used to be huts every so often along the beach where lost children should be taken. Bill went to every hut but Brian had just disappeared, and he was only four. One of the attendants at the hut put in a call to the police, who took a description and sent a police car going up and down the prom, asking through their loudspeaker if anybody had seen this child. As the minutes went into hours, we grew more and more upset. It was really a wild afternoon, with heavy rain and the waves crashing up against the wall and spilling over on to the prom. Bill was getting short-tempered, though he tried to reassure us both and our poor nephew Brian was

very subdued. The police began to go up and down the side streets where the boarding houses were, repeating their question, "Have you seen this child?" It reached a point where there was some talk of getting the lifeboat out and by five o'clock we were distraught, fearing the worst. Then a policeman came and told us a child had been taken to Layton Police Station, but not to raise our hopes in case it wasn't Brian. The police car soon had us at Layton and there sat Brian eating a huge jam butty, his face tear-streaked and his little socks and boots soaked from the rain.

Apparently two women who had been on the beach had seen Brian on his own and instead of taking him to one of the huts, as the rain had started and it was so heavy, they had taken him to their boarding house. It was only when the police started touring the streets that they took him to the police station. The sergeant wiped the floor with the two women and informed us we could press charges against them. However, we were so happy to have Brian back we didn't make any charges. It was nearly 7.00pm when we got back to the boarding house. What a day!

A change of manager at Barlows brought Bill a change of job. In those days you had to go to the union for a job and they found Bill the same type of work at a firm called Tommy Meadows on Samuel Ogden Street in Manchester. The money there was very poor, so Bill was off again. His next

Clopton Street, looking towards Hulme Hippodrome, in 1962

job was at Stewart Thomson's on Aytoun Street. At this firm Bill had to take parcels to London Road Station (now Piccadilly) and it was on one of these occasions that he saw the American film actress Kim Novak get off a train. For years afterwards he described seeing her in her fur (he pronounced it "fair") coat – honestly, you would have thought she was royalty! He told everybody about it.

It was during these years that if you went down Great Jackson Street towards Chester Road, there was a pawn shop run by Mr Harry Dutton, a lovely man. One day a man went in and Mr Dutton turned his back on him to get whatever he had asked for. When he turned back, the man was holding a gun and demanding that Mr Dutton hand over his takings. Poor Mr Dutton refused and the man shot him; sadly, Mr Dutton later died in hospital. A couple of days afterwards a man was charged with his murder.

Great Jackson Street about 1948

Then a shocking thing came to Hulme which, because it frightened me so much, stopped me going out in the evenings for a good while. If you wanted to take a short cut from Howard Street to Bedford Street you could go down the entry practically opposite our house. By doing this you would come alongside Miss Massey's newspaper and sweet shop. She was a lovely lady who had run this shop single-handed for many years. One morning as we got there, there seemed to be police all over the place. Miss Massey's shop wasn't opened and somebody had reported this

to the sergeant at the station because it was so unusual. In the shop and house nothing was out of place, but Miss Massey was nowhere to be seen. Eventually her body was found in the outside toilet; she had been strangled. Why, nobody knew. There was money in the till, as if Miss Massey had got everything ready for the day ahead, the shelves were stocked up and nothing had been taken. We were all deeply shocked at this terrible deed, the more so because she was such a nice person and was a good age. The murderer was never caught.

Towards the end of 1946 I

discovered I was to have another baby, and on Easter Saturday, April 5th 1947, I gave birth to a daughter, again in Withington Hospital and again with many problems. In fact, I remember the doctor saying to Bill, "Your wife must not have any more children; the next one will kill her." The day after I had been admitted Bill rang the ward to see how I was doing from a telephone box outside the Eagle public house on the corner of Stretford Road and Moss Lane. When he was told by the sister in charge of the ward that he had a daughter, he promptly went into the Eagle and bought everybody a drink. (No wages that week!) I was lucky to have the same doctors that I had had for Brian. I've never forgotten them. The night before I had our Maureen the nurse had to bring them to the ward. The lady doctor, Doctor Iris Spencer, arrived in her dressing gown and curlers and they were with me most of the night and the following morning until our daughter was born. I was in again for three weeks, then allowed home.

Life was starting to get back into a pattern, though the war years had left their mark upon everybody. Families had been torn apart and members of my own family had lost loved ones. Learning to live with such loss was a very hard job for some people, an impossibility for others.

Our Brian, now five, started at Duke Street School and later the same year Bill was called up to do his National Service. He

Victory party at Richards & Taylor's, Ellesmere Street, 1945

went into the RAF. Bobby, our dog, hadn't been too well for a while and Bill senior used to take him to the PDSA on Oxford Road, where they treated him for a stomach problem. But in the end they told Bill they couldn't do any more and poor old Bobby had to be put to sleep. Everybody was very upset, he was such a good little dog. Bill was in a bad way for many weeks afterwards and vowed we would never have another dog.

Maureen was just over twelve months old when we had our last holiday in Blackpool in 1948. This time it was Aunt Ada who had given us the name of a boarding house where she had once stayed. It was dreadful! The food was awful and we had booked in for bed, breakfast and evening meals. For breakfast we were given one piece of toast with a few (and I mean a few) beans on it. When I asked the woman if I could have some milk for our daughter's bottle and breakfast you would have thought I had asked for the moon! She did find us some, but I had to pay there and then for it. We would be so hungry when we came out each morning that we had to buy extra food, especially as the children had stomachs like bottomless pits, and our money soon dwindled.

Outside the boarding house there was a large grid and one morning I dropped a 2s (10p) piece which rolled down the grid. That was a lot of money in those days, so I went back inside and told the landlady what I had done. She said she could not do anything about it, as the grid would not move and she had no key for the cellar window. Amazingly, the day before we left to come home the 2s had vanished, but we never received it.

We seemed to be fated that holiday. Bill had borrowed a camera to take photographs of the children on the beach and by the middle of the week the film was used up, so we took it into a shop near the Tower to be developed. It was a lovely day, so we thought we would take the children to the beach and on the way down to the front we passed a pub called the Greyhound near to Madam Tussaud's. Outside the pub sat a small Scottie dog. Bill always patted dogs and stroked them, but this time as he stood up the dog snapped and bit into Bill's hand. We spent the next few hours in the Victoria Hospital, where Bill had his hand stitched up! Later Bill went to the pub and complained to the landlord

about the dog, but he just replied, "It was your own fault." Despite the lovely weather, what with the stingy meals at the boarding house and Bill's accident, we were quite depressed. However, we got our silver lining.

The Friday before we were due to go home we had just enough money for food and to get the film out of the shop. I waited outside while Bill went in for the photographs. He came out saying, "Hurry up, hurry up!" and rushed off down the street. I didn't understand what the rush was, but he stopped as we turned the corner of the street and explained. He had given the shopkeeper a pound note and received the photographs, but the man had given him change for £5. The shop was very full at the time and obviously the man had got confused. It was very dishonest of us but because we had no money left Bill hadn't told the man of his mistake. That extra £4 really made the day; the children went on all the rides and had a lovely time.

As the two Brians were at school, Mam had our Maureen and I returned to Barlows on a part-time basis. Well, they called it part-time! My hours were 11.00am until 6.00pm but many's the night I would still be there at 8.00pm, and we had to work every Saturday morning. Without Mam we would never have been able to manage. The two Brians went to her house from school until we came home from work and Aunt Ada's youngest daughter Mary also

went to Mam; she always had a house full of children and had remarkable patience with them all.

Our son Brian was a very quiet little boy, nothing like his cousin. He was content to sit and watch what everyone else was up to, whilst Joe's Brian was a real harum-scarum. For instance, one day I had come home at dinner time when a rag and bone man appeared in Howard Street. Joe's Brian asked if he could have a fish in the bowl that was swinging on the back of the man's cart. The rag and bone man replied, "Get me some old clothes and the fish is yours." As I only had an hour's dinner, everything was always a rush. Brian came tearing in, shouting, "Aunty Mary, Aunty Mary, can-I-have-some-old-clothes-for-the-rag-bone-man-and-he-will-give-me-a-fish?" Quite without thinking, I said, "Oh, take my coat off the door." No sooner said than done – Brian had gone, coat and all. As it was my only coat, I had to give chase, falling in the process and putting both knees through my stockings! He was forever up to little things like that, but we could always laugh after the event.

Bill and our Joe used to go to the football match each Saturday, Bill an ardent Manchester City fan and Joe a Manchester United supporter. I too had been to many football matches with Bill at home and away, but once a man was crushed to death on the railings and that put me off. The trouble was,

The Eagle, Stretford Road

Bill could only see City; no other football team was any good. So on the weeks they went to see United, Bill would cheer for the other team. Can you imagine the trouble if someone did that today? We often laughed about it.

The 1950s and 1960s

By 1948 the flats on Great Jackson Street (now Jackson Crescent) which had been begun before the war had two avenues built up. The first one was called Humberstone and the second one Hunmanby Avenue. Along the row were nine passages, each with six flats. As Howard Street was due to be demolished, Mam was offered a ground floor flat in Hunmanby Avenue. It looked lovely when we went to see it; a living room, a kitchen, two bedrooms and a bathroom. The kitchens had back to back grates and each one had a small verandah attached and a gas cooker. Mam accepted the flat, but before she could move in all her furniture had to be fumigated. She took great exception to this, saying she was not dirty, but of course it was because it was new property. Aunt Ada's house in Howard Street had to come down too and she took a house in Stamford Street, Old Trafford, where she lived for many years. She suffered from very bad arthritis and walked with the aid of a stick, but it didn't keep her in – she used to walk miles. A fine woman who had weathered all of life's knocks, she called an ace an ace and a spade a spade; if she had something to say, she would say it and if you didn't like it, that was your hard luck.

After Joe came out of the army he stayed at Mam's and in due course started courting a young woman called Ada who worked at the White Lion. Ada was a widow with three young children. On 18th September 1950 they were married and lived near Moss Lane until they moved to Chorlton-cum-Hardy. Their marriage was blessed with a daughter, whom they called Rona. We were all so pleased our Joe was happy again.

Also living in Moss Side until 1954 was Uncle Georgie, Mam's older brother by almost two years. He had been poorly for some time and Mam and I visited him regularly. He and his wife Aunt Lizzie had begun their married life in the Cambridge Street area and had moved to Moss Side, somewhere near to where Aunt Jane Hannah lived, in later years. They had three sons and two daughters, but one son died very young and that left Frank and Georgie, Betty and Ivy. Aunt Lizzie, apart from being Mam's sister-in-law, was a very good friend. Sadly, on 19th June 1954 Uncle Georgie passed away and he was buried at Southern Cemetery. The friendship between Mam and Aunt Lizzie continued for many years until, through age, they were no longer able to visit each other. Aunt Lizzie passed away on 22nd April 1969 and was laid to rest with Uncle Georgie.

When our present Queen was crowned in 1953, the neighbours collected once more and street parties were organised all over Hulme. As Brian and Maureen spent most of the time at Mam's because Bill and I were working, they attended the party in Humberstone Avenue. Everybody worked so hard: the bunting went from verandah to verandah all along the avenues and so did the tables. The flats were called Bentley House; anyone familiar with these avenues will know how long they are and be able to imagine what a sight all the decorations made. Nearly every flat had a Union Jack and a poster of the Queen in the window. After the party all the children were taken to Lime Park and each child received a decorated mug with details of the coronation on it. Again a lovely day for both adults and children.

Our son Brian left Duke Street in 1954 after passing his eleven plus examination. He went on to St Margaret's School in Moss Side and later to Openshaw Technical College, passing all his examinations to qualify as a draughtsman in later years. As Brian and

Mary and Bill Jordan, son Brian, daughter Maureen and nephew Brian in Blackpool, 1948

Maureen were growing up, Bill and I took them to the pictures every Friday evening. We would meet Bill from work and go to any of the five main picture houses in Manchester centre: the Gaumont, Oxford, Theatre Royal, Deansgate or the Regal. Even now they can recall many films they saw years ago. As they grew older, first Brian stopped coming with us, then Maureen, but when our grand-children came along we started the cycle all over again.

One evening I had finished work and called at Mam's to collect our Maureen, only to find her flat had been flooded out. The rain had been so heavy that the drains on the verandah could not take the amount of water and it had come in under the door to the kitchen, in no time washing through the entire flat. Mam

One of the architects' impressions of the new Hulme

had tried her best to move things, but without success, even though all the neighbours

were helping. The skirting boards were about 5 inches deep and the water at some point had been above them. Mam lost most of her carpets and some of her furniture. Some weeks later, Manchester Corporation sent workmen to all the ground floor flats to knock out a couple of bricks in the verandah walls, presumably to stop it happening again. After many hours of mopping up and sorting things out I went home, only to find my own front bedroom flooded. Earlier that day my landlord had sent workmen to put new cords in all my windows and on finishing the job they had left the bedroom window open. More mopping up! I had to report what had happened to the landlord, but I regretted it. The poor men lost their jobs because, as he put it, "they had slipshod ways". I felt very sorry for them.

In June 1958 Bill married a girl called Norma from Wythenshawe. They bought a house and moved to Sale. Their marriage took place in St Wilfrid's Church, but not the one in Hulme; this was another church in Northenden. There were so many weddings around that time it was nice, so many good things were happening. Our Joe's son Brian was already married. One year after Bill's wedding my sister Edna's eldest daughter June got married at St Bride's Church in Old Trafford and a couple of years after that her sister Edna was also wed there. It was like turning the pages of a book. One minute all our children were small and now they were all marrying, a whole new generation springing up.

In 1958 it was our Brian's turn to leave school, for he was sixteen years old. He got a job with Lancashire Tar Distillers

Homes for Heroes

Few houses have hot water, baths or electricity. Many were scheduled for demolition before the war, now blast-shaken, often damp and unsafe, they have to serve a further term of years

Some housewives yield to the difficulties and give up the unequal struggle, but many homes are scrubbed and cleaned and polished, and shine the equal of any in the land

❖ ❖ ❖

Homes for Heroes—they have to be heroes—and most of them are

Part of the post-war campaign for re-housing in Hulme

in Warrington, in the drawing office, and this is where he learnt to become a draughtsman. Because of the distance he had to travel we bought him a bike (much against my better judgement). He certainly did some pedalling those weeks! The bike shop was on the corner of Stretford Road and Clopton Street. One day whilst at work Brian had stripped and cleaned his bike, only to find when he had finished work that someone had stolen it. There was still a sum left to pay on it and even though we told the man at the bike shop what had happened, we had to continue the payments. But in some ways I was glad; one was always reading of accidents, especially in Trafford Park, and that was the way Brian used to go to work.

In 1962 our daughter Maureen left school and started work as an office junior at Ferranti Ltd, West Gorton. Our Brian had got married the year before and this year we got our first grandchild. She was christened Maureen, a delightful little girl who as soon as she could talk could chatter away nineteen to the dozen. Our Joe and Edna were already grandparents, so now it was our turn. 1964 brought our first grandson, christened David; as he grew he had all the makings of a right scallywag! Both children did very well at school, gaining many O Levels and both securing good jobs.

In 1963 Oswald Street too came under the hammer and was due to be demolished. Mam would not give up her flat and live with any of us and because of her age I didn't leave Hulme. Bill and I moved into a flat.

Many memories, happy and sad, were housed within those walls at Oswald Street and it was awful having to leave, but we had no choice. My life had always been hard and heavy going, as had Bill's, but we had had more than most people could ever have wished for.

Aunt Ada passed away in January 1965 and this really shattered Mam. I don't feel she ever fully came to terms with it. Aunt Ada was so much younger than Mam and they had both been through so much together, comforted and consoled each other, and laughed and cried at so many things in their lifetime. It was like the beginning of the end. Mam was now the last one left from a family of twelve children. Aunt Ada was buried at Weaste Cemetery, just in front of my dad's grave, with Uncle Tom and our cousin Edna.

Moving house was like starting all over again. There was only our Maureen left to be married now and time was marching on.

Into the Present

In the December of 1972 our Edna's husband Harry died very unexpectedly. He was buried in Southern Cemetery and at his funeral a Scots piper led the mourners and played "Amazing Grace"; it was very upsetting. No sooner were we getting over that shock than Mam left this world, aged almost 87 years, in April 1973. Her loss to me could never be explained, for she had helped each and every one of the entire family in one way or another. A truly wonderful lady, much loved and respected,

Daughter Maureen

and one who had always put the needs of others in front of her own. Mam was laid to rest at Weaste Cemetery with our beloved father. It was like the end of an era for me.

How quickly the years pass! Our daughter Maureen had married in 1967 at St Philip's Church (now demolished for the Mancunian Way). Her husband Vic came from a family who lived opposite us and at the time of their marriage he was serving in the Royal Navy. They gave us our third grandchild in 1975, a little boy they had christened Stuart.

Our children all now married and three lovely grandchildren – what more could we want? Bill and I looked after all of them whilst their parents were at work. Bill loved all his grandchildren and, as when his own children were small, his patience was endless; they in turn adored their grandad.

One morning I had the radio on and a request came on from a lady who wanted to get in touch with anybody who had worked at Barlows Ltd. The lady said her name was Mrs Rose Lyons and she wanted these people to write to her. I wondered if she could be the girl called Rosie May who had left Barlows during the war years. I did write and lo and behold, it was the same person! Numerous letters have since passed between us and as Rose kept in touch with Elsie Smith (now Lowe) I am now writing to and receiving mail from Australia. How lovely it was to catch up with each other's lives! All three of us now look forward to receiving each other's letters.

Oswald Street in 1961